# Baby Boomers to Generation Z:
## Capitalizing on generational diversity to grow a successful law firm

BY DAVID LAUD

**Head of events and books**
Leah Darbyshire

**Commissioning editor**
Alex Davies

**Published by**
Globe Law and Business Ltd
3 Mylor Close
Horsell
Woking
Surrey GU21 4DD
United Kingdom
Tel: +44 20 3745 4770
www.globelawandbusiness.com

ISBN: 978-1-78358-376-8
A catalogue record for this book is available from the British Library

# Contents

# Executive summary

In this current period of the 21st century, our workplace is more diverse than at any other point in time. This diversity is due to a broadening ethnic mix, gender representation, and spread of generations. Greater mobility, socio economic and legislative developments account in the most part for the first two factors, but what of the third? What has caused this widening of the generational spectrum in the workplace?

Historically in law firms, the older generation, in particular partners, would move toward retirement and hand over the reins to the next oldest. In today's world of work, with improved healthcare, increased life expectancy, greater knowledge of fitness, and in part historic anxiety over the effects of the global recession, there's a reluctance to rush to retirement.

Specifically here we're talking about the Baby Boomer generation, who are aged between 55 and 73 and, as the name suggests, are not in short supply. Typically schooled in a traditional hierarchical command management style they are the generation now most often faced with tackling the integration of disruptive and aspirational Gen X'ers and more technologically adept and collaborative (but considered less driven) Gen Y or Millennials. They're also now seeing the newest arrivals, Gen Z, who bring an even greater affinity to everything digital but are not quite so comfortable with matters of an interpersonal nature.

It's quite a challenge, and the reason why this publication delves into the differences between the generations, their influences, preferences, strengths and weaknesses, to better understand and thereby manage the staff who fall into the respective age groupings.

The consequence of older generations remaining in post is a fascinating and yet challenging prospect. Law firms can be presented with the task of managing at least four and sometimes five different age groups. It becomes five if we add those fit and able and working who are in their mid-70s and beyond, who belong to the "silent generation".

Multiple generations in one practice with the oldest holding on to the power base and ownership can create pressure points for younger, ambitious professionals seeking a stake rather than simply a "steady job". It's likely that in many law firms those appealing for a place at the partners' table will now be coming from Generation Y or Millennials aged in their early to late 30s. Millennials are considered more focused on experiences outside of work than within, but this does not hide or diminish their need for recognition and reward. Gen X'ers will mostly be in their 40s and early 50s and the majority of this group will already have established their partnership credentials.

In other words, if it was going to happen for them, it's likely to have been handled one way or another. The X'ers are something of a filling in the career sandwich, with slices of Millennial below and Boomer above. There is a smaller population of Generation X and they will need to find appropriate skills and knowledge to work with their younger and older generational colleagues for mutual gain.

By 2020, 50 percent of the US workforce will be made up of Millennial or the "Y" Generation; by 2030 it will be 75 percent. These Millennial employees, born between 1980 and 1996, have ridden several seismic waves of change – from political and environmental to communication and technological innovation – and this pace of change shows little sign of abating.

Having experienced an ever more connected, digitally-driven world, Millennials are now moving through firms to take greater responsibility, head teams, run departments or entire businesses, and in certain cases creating their own version of a law firm.

This book explores the various generations within law firms and the challenges, threats, and opportunities they face as staff deal with colleagues from younger or older groups, be they Baby Boomer or Generations X, Y (Millennial) or the next wave of "Z's" as they enter the world of work. The structure of the book takes the reader through a life-cycle of a lawyer from qualification and first seat through to partnership and business ownership.

We must start our journey of discovery by better understanding the experiences and needs of the generations.

Generational diversity raises interesting questions for those managing the business and specifically individuals responsible for hiring, training, supervising, and leading within the firm.

Here are eight examples of queries that the generational divide may prompt:

- Do we need to adapt our recruitment policies and procedures to attract candidates from different generational groups?
- Is our training meeting the needs of our employees across each generation and learning style?
- Are we communicating effectively with clients from diverse generational groups or are we simply offering each the same options?
- Do our staff receive training in interpersonal skills and management that reflects the diversity in generations?
- Are we aware of the staff who have active side hustles and are we engaged with them?
- What do we know about our staff interests outside of the workplace?
- Have we identified and nurtured our next group of leaders within the firm?
- How do we work at retaining the interest and loyalty of our staff?

Mindful of the danger of over generalization, it is true to note that Millennials have become the most studied generation of all time, and gaining a better understanding of traits, tendencies, and beliefs of ALL generations can significantly assist those responsible for leading, growing, and managing succession within organizations.

The legal sector is under increasing pressure to evolve and adapt to the changing world. Despite the rise in technological solutions, including AI and smart contracts, law firms remain heavily reliant on their human resources. Without an appreciation of increasing generational diversity and their inherent challenges, firms will continue to struggle. One further – and many would argue critical – example rests with the perennial issue of succession and encouraging the next wave of "bright young things" to take the responsibility of managing the future of the business.

For this succession process to work, a firm requires a strong cohort of suitably qualified, engaged, motivated, and committed practitioners. Arriving at that point requires preparation, planning, and effective implementation of management initiatives that acknowledge the needs of that cohort's generation.

By following the path from sourcing, onboarding, training, developing, and leadership development, this book provides suggestions and thought-provoking content to help forward-thinking firms better manage their age-diverse personnel.

# About the author

David Laud is a management consultant who provides strategic support for law firms around the world. David's career in the legal sector started over 20 years ago and included 14 years as the chief executive of a successful UK firm. He has a master's degree in marketing and is a fellow of the Chartered Institute of Marketing.

He gained his early management experience with global travel company, Thomas Cook, where he was responsible for the introduction of an innovative range of travel guides and led an international project team to build a successful new money transfer product, MoneyGram, subsequently sold to Travelex for $65m.

David has published articles on law firm management in *The Lawyer*, the *Law Society Gazette* and *Legal Practice Management* and also regularly appears on BBC radio and TV.

He lives in England with his wife, Jo, and has three children, Georgie, Ellie and Bob, collectively known as Gellibob.

# Chapter 1: Generations explained

From the outset it's important to note that generational variances are derived from a number of known factors and it's not as simple as grouping people by their age and expecting identical behaviors.

In the workplace we can often find it difficult to relate to younger or older colleagues and have trouble putting our finger on the cause for this communication breakdown.

One factor that can have a frequent impact on intergenerational communication and collaboration in the workplace is quite simple and logical. At any particular time in our lives we will have specific needs, aspirations and beliefs At the outset we want to land a job with the right firm and prospects for development. Outside of work we may still live with parents, have little by way of commitments, other than college or university fees. Contrast this with the 40-something lawyer who has a mortgage, is divorced and has two children. Here the commitments are manifold and priorities in life may err toward "safety" rather than risk. Again, consider how the 40-something outlook compares to the 65-year-old senior partner who has declared she is retiring in a year's time. She is married, has four grandchildren and a beach house in Malibu. In recent years the senior partner has taken on non-executive director posts with several charities and is an active fundraiser. Ok, so this is a clear generalization, some may say stereotyping, of three distinct ages in the workplace, but when we are at different points in our lives we do see things differently and this can often spill out in conflict, confusion or, at worst, mistrust of colleagues.

We may have a sense of urgency that isn't shared, or a predilection for risk that others find uncomfortable. Our priority may be income security over altruism or promotion over happiness, taking on a role that you're not ready for and ultimately becoming over stressed.

So where we are in our lives plays an obvious part in how we see ourselves and colleagues, but there are also the events that we've encountered in the past that will potentially influence our thinking.

By way of example, one such influential circumstance could be a major event and its impact at a key developmental period, such as witnessing the first manned landing on the moon or the devastating sight of events on 9/11. Such events can have a far-reaching impact on individuals, affecting behavioral responses to factors such as views on finances, job security and relationship with authority figures.

As humans we are infinitely complex beings and it would be wrong to suggest the following analysis as definitive traits as depicted for each group. What we can take from this analysis is the knowledge that personality, intelligence, wellbeing etc. are all factors that influence an individual's approach to work but our generational "tribe" tendencies can also offer up some very useful insights.

In short, we can be certain that generational analysis – whilst more scientific than a horoscope – should not be used rigidly to compartmentalize a generation or define an individual. As with most aspects of our make-up, there are often exceptions to rules and factors that simply don't register where they may for a majority. There will also be a crossover of typologies at the start and end points of any given period of generational grouping.

This chapter defines the different generations within the workplace, presenting an analysis of the most obvious and defined traits.

I know that the Generation X analysis is close to my own outlook and manner of working but not 100 percent accurate. No doubt as you review each generation you will see elements that you can recognize as one of your own traits, yet falls within another group.

How you use this information will be for you to decide; however, it can offer up a supportive guide to forming plans to:

- Better engage with prospective candidates;
- Nurture and retain talent within the firm;
- Motivate and obtain greater productivity;
- Create a positive culture and happy workplace;
- Improve creative and strategic thinking;
- Identify potential leaders and future partners; and
- Secure business succession and the future of the firm.

Here follows a snapshot of commonly understood traits of the most populous generations within most law firms.

With the youngest of the Silent Generation now in their mid-70s it is a reasonable assumption that most will be enjoying retirement; however, an ageing population does offer up the potential of some working on well into their 80s. For the purpose of this book, our analysis extends to the following main generational groups.

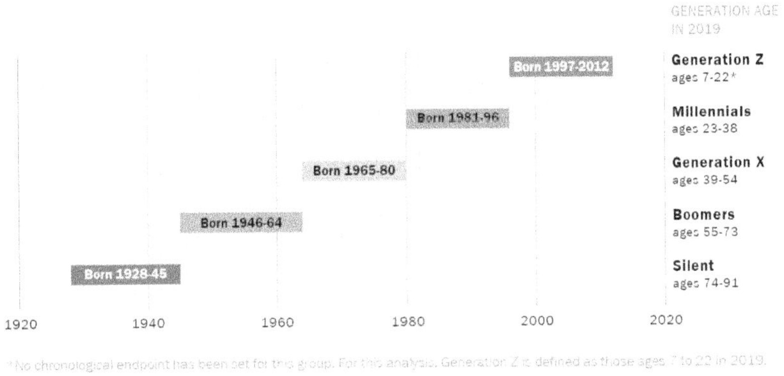


*Figure 1: The generations defined. Source: Pew Research Center.*

## Baby boomers: 1946–1964

- I am motivated and hard-working and generally team orientated;
- I will challenge authority;
- My engagement with technology will vary from developer to abstainer;
- I seek recognition for my achievements;
- I can have workaholic tendencies; and
- Work tends to define me.

## Generation X: 1965–1980

- I work smart, not necessarily hard;
- Don't micro-manage me;
- Technology doesn't frighten me but I'm careful not to be governed by it;
- I tend to be a problem solver and adapt well to change;

- Tell me what to do and I'll show you how;
- I generally have very high expectations; and
- Family and financial care are important to me.

**Generation Y (Millennials): 1981–1996**

- I am career-motivated but not necessarily loyal to my employer;
- I want to work with you, not for you;
- I require support but often respond well to structured mentoring;
- I seek a sense of community within the workplace;
- I have high expectations;
- I am productive and efficient when supplied with the resources and guidance; and
- Friends are important and the need to be liked.

**Generation Z: 1997–present**

- Connectivity and my networks are very important to me;
- I keep up with technology and mostly operate at an advanced level compared to older colleagues;
- Manual and multiple sources of information frustrate me; I want to access everything from one device;
- I need to be kept informed and know my responses are noted; and
- Compared to other generations I will spend proportionately more time searching for and changing jobs.

Here below are examples of major events that possibly influenced the respective generations.

Please note that whilst these events have occurred in defined timelines, there are clear areas of overlap. For example, all generations have been affected by social media but it has had its greatest influence over the generation that first embraced it, the Millennials. There are strong signals from Generation Z that social media platforms are no longer "cool" and investigations into the efficacy of the companies running the sites are proving their instincts to be well founded.

| | Baby Boomers | Gen X | Gen Y (Millennial) | Gen Z |
|---|---|---|---|---|
| **Born** | 1946–64 | 1965–80 | 1981–96 | 1997– |
| **Events** | Cold War/ Berlin Wall<br>Everest climbed<br>Rock 'n' Roll/ Beatles<br>Woodstock<br>Birth control<br>Sputnik/Moon landing<br>JFK / Dr King<br>Civil rights<br>Vietnam<br>Watergate | AIDS<br>Punk rock<br>Reagan/ Thatcher<br>Falklands War<br>Lady Diana<br>Chernobyl<br>The internet<br>Ethiopian famine<br>Berlin Wall destroyed<br>Mandela released<br>Gulf war<br>Clinton impeachment<br>Columbine High School massacre | School shootings<br>Rap music<br>Social media<br>9/11<br>Barrack Obama<br>Putin<br>*Harry Potter*<br>The euro<br>Amazon | ISIS<br>President Trump<br>Cambridge Analytica<br>Crowdfunding<br>Smartphone<br>Cyclone Idai<br>Brexit<br>Global warming |
| **Parental influence** | Wartime experiences<br>Rationing of food and resources<br>Mother kept house whilst father worked | First generation where more common for both parents to work<br>High divorce rate amongst parents | Parents' greater involvement in child develop-ment/ security | Parents having an increased awareness of technology but still far behind this generation |
| **Technology** | Landline phone<br>Fax<br>Email<br>Dictaphone<br>Internet | Email<br>Cell phone<br>SMS text/cell text<br>Internet | Email<br>Text<br>Cell phone/text<br>Smartphone<br>Laptop | Smartphone<br>Text<br>Messaging apps<br>Apps over web<br>VR/AI |
| **Positive traits** | Hard working<br>Team players | Flexible and able to think laterally | Tech capable<br>Community focus/ethical | Tech advanced<br>Desire to stay up to date |
| **Negative traits** | Rigid thinking/ intolerance | Dislike of hierarchy/ disruptive | Requires clear guidelines<br>Expectations often outweigh reality | Inability to concentrate/ easily distracted |

# Chapter 2: Recruitment – securing the best talent

Most firms will have their own well-rehearsed and trusted forms of onboarding talent. These processes, with perhaps the exception of internships, will follow a standard pattern. If this approach has worked for the business and to date not resulted in a negative event, you may have found the ideal formula. More likely, the experience in the legal sector is a mix of success and failure, which can be hard to predict and subsequently costly and highly frustrating.

Recent research undertaken by Oxford Economics put the cost of replacing within the sector at $52,000 (£39,000). That's simply the cost to replace before you consider the salary. Those costs can be attributed to recruitment agency fees and the additional salary paid to a locum lawyer recruited to temporarily keep the post afloat.

There is no shortage of aspiring lawyers acquiring their law degree; in fact so many that a large number end up as baristas rather than barristers. So why is it so difficult to find a replacement when someone quits, or hire a suitably experienced lawyer to cope with demand in an area of growth?

The reality is that, like many other sectors, the legal world responds to market and economic conditions generating trends in demand that directly affect the supply of the required talent and experience.

Consider the impact of the 2008 recession, where the cause – subprime mortgage lending – resulted in an aftershock of fiscal control directly impacting the demand for a wide range of legal services, both personal and commercial. As a consequence, law firms looked to their overheads and reduced their headcount to survive. Over the next ten years the legal sector slowly began to recover, but practices large and small remained wary of over investing in fear of a repeat of the pain in 2008.

Areas that were considered risky or returning too little profit were often the focal point for the cuts, and, as this move took hold across the profession, those lawyers impacted adjusted and retrained in areas of greater demand. More experienced lawyers either retired or quit the legal world to pursue other opportunities and newly qualified lawyers decided from the outset to specialize elsewhere. Once a recovery started to recreate a demand in these areas, the much-needed expertise was no longer available, resulting in considerable difficulty for a large number of firms and very healthy remuneration packages for those few hardy souls who had survived the recessionary storms and were still able to offer the once unpopular legal service.

Supply and demand, economic impact, legislative change, technological advancement, artificial intelligence and yes, generational preferences, all come into the equation when recruiting. To be successful you need to consistently deliver on the recruitment brief and be aware of pitfalls and opportunities to ensure you retain that healthy flow of talent within your firm.

As a partner, director, manager or CEO it is important to learn from common recruitment and onboarding mistakes. Of equal importance is the ability to retain a focus on those positive characteristics you should actively seek to add real value through the hiring process.

The following are not defined by generational variances but will hopefully resonate with anyone who has held responsibility for recruitment and act as reminders of the good and not so good sides of the challenge.

## The good

You should actively seek out those who show:

- **They know your firm** and have actively expressed an interest in joining, demonstrating their alignment with your beliefs and culture;
- **Passion but in a positive way**. Without getting out of hand the candidate has drive and energy that seems infectious. They're a natural doer who can prove they deliver;
- **Emotional intelligence**. There's a lot of discussion on this topic and for good reason. In a world dominated by technology and online networks there's great value in finding someone who can engage meaningfully one-to-one or one-to-many. They demonstrate that they are empathetic and an effective listener as well as an effective communicator. Pick the right one and you could have just hired your future managing partner;

- **The mentor**. With age can come very valuable experience. Those who come to your firm with a few grey hairs and miles on the clock can be a real asset but only if they're prepared to share the benefit of that hard-won experience. Mentoring is a skill and it's not for everyone, but if an older candidate expresses interest in such an added responsibility it's a good sign; and
- **The team player**. Hollywood loves to portray the "lone wolf" style of lawyer but in the real world an effective attorney these days needs to work in a team and make sure they collaborate effectively. If your candidate can demonstrate the attributes of a strong team player they'll fit well into most organizations.

### The bad

Avoid:

- **Being held to ransom** for a big paycheck and benefits package that will have a consequential negative impact within the firm (as much as you might want your team not to share salary information, trust me they will);
- **Compromising** too far with a candidate who falls short on qualification, experience, references, terms (in particular their hours if it won't cover client needs), marketability, and attitude (see toxic below);
- **Over spec** by offering the job to an over-qualified and very experienced candidate when the role suits someone more junior. This can work but only when the candidate is clearly advised and accepts the scope of the role and that it isn't a gateway position to re-boot their career;
- **The serial job hopper** – usually a quick glance at a candidate's CV will highlight their "stick-ability" when it comes to their career. If you're looking at a resume with as many as four different employers within a six- to ten-year period, you could be looking at a serial hopper. Typically, they start positively but when the honeymoon flush of the new role starts to fade, so does their enthusiasm. Often the thrill of the chase of a new opportunity aligned to the ego boost of attention and ultimately selection provides such a rush they can't wait for their next hit. Don't fall for it unless you're prepared to see the churn of your firm increase; and

- Introducing **toxic talent**. At times in the recruitment process you and colleagues may have that eyebrow raising moment when a stray comment or considered response jars. Attitude is mentioned above; however, this is such a crucial area it is worthy of its own section. On paper and in the most part in person the individual may present as the ideal candidate, some may say perfect but... there are personality traits and views that do not sit with the culture of the firm. From experience I advocate in the strongest possible terms to "follow your gut", trust your instincts and don't hire. As good a lawyer as they may be, if toxic they have the potential to upset many loyal and hardworking members of your team. The consequential cost to the business could be far greater than any benefit gained from hiring them.

All the above may sound logical and mostly in line with your approach, but how does it relate to the generational differences?

Each generation of candidates will have a preferred method of presenting themselves to the job market and equally have differing motivations and needs. As the recruiter, if you pitch a "one size fits all" approach to each and every job you'll likely have limited success. By tailoring an approach to meet the generational style of engagement, you'll not only increase your level of responses but in so doing the opportunity of finding the very best fit for your firm increases.

| | Baby Boomers | Gen X | Gen Y (Millennial) | Gen Z |
|---|---|---|---|---|
| **Available talent pool**<br>The younger members of the Silent Generation (1928–45) still feature in the work-place. US Census Bureau data 2017 recorded 3 million in work or 2 percent of the total. The youngest in 2019 will be 74. | US Census Bureau data 2017: A total of 41m (25 percent) BB in the workforce.<br>As this generation enters retirement age, the numbers decrease from the once dominant position of 66m in 1997. In 2019, the youngest Boomer is 55 years old and the oldest Boomers are 73. | US Census Bureau data 2017: A total of 53m (33 percent) Gen X in the workforce, down from a 2008 peak of 54m.<br>In 2019, the youngest Gen X will be 39 and the oldest 54. | US Census Bureau data 2017: A total of 56m (34 percent) Millennials in the workforce.<br>In 2019, the youngest Millennials will be 23 and the oldest 38.<br>Currently the strongest stock of the generations and considered to be best educated. (Pew Research) | US Census Bureau data 2017: A total of 9m (6 percent) Gen Z in the workforce.<br>In 2019, Gen Z employees will be no older than 22.<br>Bureau of Labor Statistics projects a 5.6 percent increase in legal sector jobs by 2024. Demand for a career in law has not abated. |
| **Timescales** | Candidates tend to take their time to respond, preferring phone calls and face-to-face engagement. | As with BB, Gen X can, in cases of executive selection, be prone to long deliberation. | Decisions can be made rather quicker with Millennials, although beware the counter offers. | Enthusiasm and grasp of multiple means to communicate can facilitate a swift turnaround in Gen Z selection. |
| **Attracting the talent** | Traditional routes such as signing up with a recruit-ment agent. Study job pages of legal press. Use LinkedIn but not always active. | A trend to move away from agents but they still play a part. Increasingly using LinkedIn and job sites. | Google search to source opportunities, research firms, job sites, Twitter and to a lesser extent LinkedIn used to help make decisions once job identified. | Key word alerts set to notify of suitable opportunities. |

| | Baby Boomers | Gen X | Gen Y (Millennial) | Gen Z |
|---|---|---|---|---|
| **Management of resources – HR briefing and job specification** | Play to the knowledge and experience required – likely to require suitable executive search agency with expertise in the field you have a vacancy to fill. Make full use of the internal network and alumni. Likely the role may be senior such as head of department. As such the field will be narrow and candidates not always easy to attract.<br>Post role in journals (hardcopy and online). | A key trigger here could be career progression – give careful consideration to use of recruitment agency.<br>Select jobsites that Google sources from.<br>Post the opportunity on LinkedIn and of course your own firm's website.<br>As with the BB suggestion, senior hires will always require a greater level of discretion and consideration. | Whilst there's no shortage of Gen Y lawyers their motivations and methods do differ from previous generations.<br>Online advertising is important as is the use of internal, informal networks to help identify suitable candidates to approach directly. | Give thought to presenting the community culture and diversity of your firm.<br>An online representation of the role is essential. Social media sites will also help raise the awareness of the role. Twitter, LinkedIn and to a lesser extent Facebook. |
| **Benchmarking**<br>With all cases of recruitment it is important to manage expectations and balance attracting talent with the remuneration packages currently on offer for equivalent employees. | Salary and benefits important, notably medical and pension.<br>Status and authority are important factors. | Salary and benefits important, notably medical and pension.<br>Job title and responsibilities are important factors. | Salary as ever an important consideration but also the ambition of the firm and where they will be seen within it.<br>Recognition and progression are important factors. | Salary features but overall package will be the deciding factor.<br>Ethical, ecological, diverse and responsible approach is important. |
| **Interviews** | Like structure and tradition. Will appreciate a formal style of interview and questioning style as it will be familiar. | Will not be put off by a formal approach but more likely to adapt to more unconventional, conversational approaches. | Could be turned off by a rigid, formal approach. Preference for informal, relaxed interviews with a level of structure. | Will be turned off by rigid formal interviews. Will respond well to informal, relaxed conversations and engagement. |

| | Baby Boomers | Gen X | Gen Y (Millennial) | Gen Z |
|---|---|---|---|---|
| **Candidate analysis**<br>Note: Psychometric tests should be a mixture of personality, preference and competence and tailored to the specific role. | Psychometric tests (note may be experienced in handling/ managing traditional tests), references and proof of performance. | As with BB, Gen X may have a game plan with established test types. References and proof of performance. Social media footprint. | Psychometric testing may create anxiety if not familiar with techniques. Will require careful briefing to manage expectations and reduce stress. Proof of past performance and online presence mapped. | Psychometric testing may create anxiety if not familiar with techniques. Will require careful briefing to manage expectations and reduce stress. Proof of past performance and online presence mapped. |
| **Making the offer** | Ideally face-to-face or at least a phone call to convey the job offer. This provides an ideal opportunity to gauge response and identify any potential negative issues that may hinder the hiring process.<br>Many agents suggest they convey the offer; as the employer you should insist on taking the lead. | As with BB, personal contact is preferred to stay attuned to the micro expression or vocal signals and behaviors. | Avoid their preferred email or text communication bias.<br><br>Call the successful candidate or suggest facetime or skype. | As with the previous examples, make the communication personal. Messenger apps are great but you'll be far more effective and learn more of their genuine interest by making direct contact. |
| **Closing the deal**<br>Points of negotiation | Salary<br>Pension<br>Medical | Salary<br>Job title,<br>Pension, Medical | Salary<br>The scope of role<br>Progression prospects | Salary<br>The scope of role<br>Progression prospects |

## The roles

The table highlights certain potential differentiating factors between generations during the recruitment process. When reviewing any process that involves human interaction and decision-making, the potential variances and nuances can be endless. With recruitment such factors as career stage, skills, experience, ambition etc. will all play a part.

As a consequence, it is of course impossible to state definitively which roles each generation will be pursuing at any particular point in time. Even our newest group, the Gen Z's, will be a mixture of academically gifted and those who present stronger softer skills such as emotional intelligence.

Given the above stated limitations in offering a defined list of jobs by generations, the following outline suggests strategic approaches based on the generational groupings.

### Baby Boomers

Broadly speaking, legally qualified staff who are 55+ will be seeking security and often a sideways move, offering greater career longevity.

#### Case example

Your firm is looking to add instant gravitas in an area where historically you've had no track record of success. The partners have agreed a strategic goal to identify and recruit a known individual with reputation and a following.

Searching within LinkedIn and your own trusted networks it would be entirely possible to draw up a shortlist of candidates and set a plan to attract the best match for your needs. Alternatively, or in addition, you can brief an executive search consultant to undertake the exercise on your behalf, which has the upside of providing a discrete distance between your firm and the process, but on the downside will cost, with no guarantee of success.

Don't be oversold a candidate by an agent, and don't fall into the trap of compromising, slipping from plan A to plan F, and recruiting someone who only meets 30 percent of your ideal criteria. If the right candidates are not available, the back-up plan, albeit a medium- to longer-term solution, should be to develop your own talent pool.

## Generation X

With an age range of 39–54, these lawyers will have established themselves in their career with the youngest having over 15 years' post-qualification experience. Why would they be looking to move? Frustration at lack of progression, clock ticking and no tap on the shoulder for that "partnership talk"; others promoted above them with less experience. Or simply moving to a new location as their partner has a new job.

### Case example

You have a very busy thriving real estate department and the head of section has been successful at building the business. What's not working is the operational management. Whilst fees are growing year on year, the complaints have also started to increase, turnover of staff in the department is high, and internally you have no capacity to help manage the situation.

The executive team meet and decide to recruit a lawyer with 10+ years' experience of running a successful real estate department, not yet partner but an individual who could become one within a relatively short period, if successful.

LinkedIn/Google searches and discussions with trusted contacts will highlight where the process might want to focus. An executive search specialist who knows the real estate market inside out would be very useful. Create a defined job brief for the agent and include a role specification with clear "must have" requirements.

## Millennials

The largest grouping in the workforce and the first generation to emerge having grown up with technology. Aged between 23 and 38, they will range from being just qualified to well on their way to establishing their careers.

### Case example

The firm's chief human resources officer has handed in her notice and has a three-month notice period. She will be joining a competitor law firm and as a consequence the partnership board wants to move quickly to replace and not hold her to her full notice period. Certain members of the partnership board have expressed concerns over confidentiality, remuneration and strategic plans.

Ideally you would want to recruit at this level for someone with legal sector experience; however, the pool for such an individual in your location is not large.

This poses quite a challenge but is not insurmountable. A little lateral thought can help in such circumstances. Taking the heat out of finding the ideal candidate in record time can be achieved by seeking an experienced interim HR executive. Many millennials have adapted to a portfolio working career and like the flexibility of working a series of varied assignments. It should therefore prove far easier to locate an interim replacement for six months, which will allow time for a more thorough and hopefully fruitful search for a long-term replacement.

It's always concerning when senior members of the firm leave and a worry that it may impact the morale of others; this is especially true of smaller practices where it is likely they will have close relationships with a large number of staff. Swift and decisive action will help steady any nerves and a strong interim in place may help not only fill the gap but also provide useful suggestions to improve HR practices.

## Generation Z

These guys may be the new kids on the block and come in no older than 22, but having grown up in a world more connected and advanced than ever before, they're far from being naïve.

### Case example

The intellectual property section of your firm has just won a major tender bid to work with a large tech business. The partner in charge of the department has said he is short of resource and now this new contract will require at least two, possibly three, new paralegals.

The role of a paralegal can be a career choice for many who prefer the back office, research and admin side of law. It can also be a very useful stepping stone and valuable experience for an aspiring lawyer who may or may not have a law degree.

Noting the area of work and the client, the executive team sanctions the hiring of two paralegals and specifically suggest they are recent college graduates.

Here's an opportunity to talk to your local college and enquire as to any recent graduates looking for such opportunities. There's no need to involve fee-charging third parties – a well-drafted job ad posted with the popular vacancy sites, along with discussions amongst staff and trusted networks, will typically generate enough interest to provide a healthy interest in the opportunities.

## Statistical data

Below are supporting statistical data highlighting the population size by generation, education, and income split.

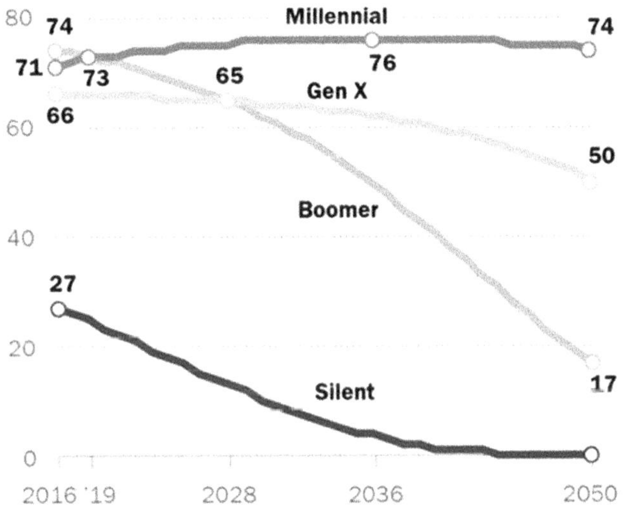


*Figure 1: Projected population by generations (in millions). Source: Pew Research Center: Analysis of US Census Bureau population projections released December 214 and 2016 population estimates.*

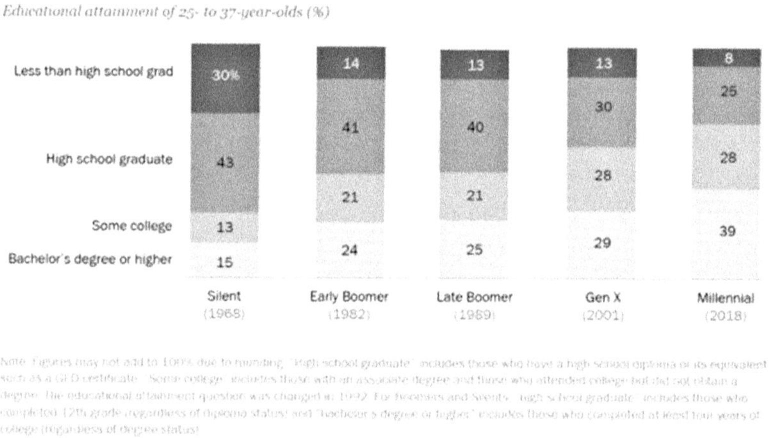


*Figure 2: Millennials and education vs other generations. Source: Pew Research Center: analysis of 1968, 1982, 2001 and 2018 current population survey annual social and economic supplements (IPUMS).*

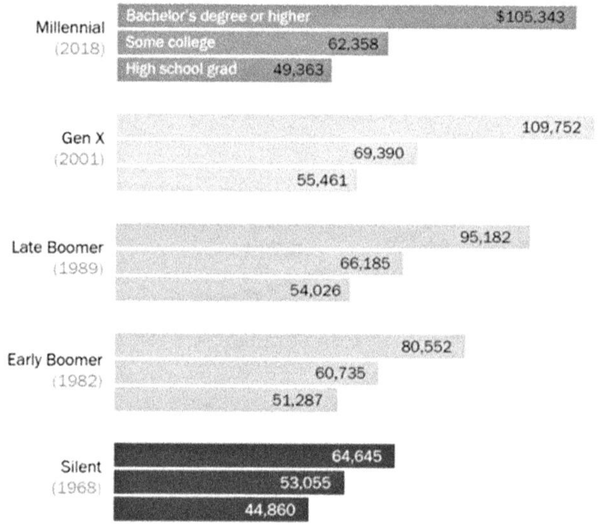


*Figure 3: Education and income gaps. Source: Pew Research Center*

A recent report by DeLoitte also highlights the priorities of younger generations and how they can be at odds with the culture of a prospective employer. This is covered in more detail in chapter four.

# Chapter 3: Training and development

Having successfully recruited your candidates, they will need to be inducted to your firm and its culture. Successful legal practices invest considerable resource, time, and cost in sharing knowledge and keeping their teams and specialists up to date with essential developments. It's therefore important to understand how an appreciation of generational differences and preferences can help improve the effectiveness of learning for recipients.

Baby Boomers grew up in an era where "talk and chalk" were the standard order of the day. Lawyers of this generation will have considerable experience of sitting in lectures listening to speakers deliver words of wisdom whilst furiously making undecipherable notes. Of course, the experience of lecture-led learning will not always have been negative and BB's will point to professors who entertained their audiences whilst delivering all important information.

Not exposed to technology such as computers until post-qualification and typically working for a number of years, the Baby Boomers have had quite an adjustment to make and many still find webinars and apps an anathema.

Generation X'ers by contrast became familiar with computers at school and college, making the transition to the workplace that much easier. There is a challenging side to the X generation, often translating into verbal interventions when lectures or study fail to live up to expectations. This disruptive nature is at odds with the traditional approach of the previous generation, often those delivering the lessons.

In the workplace, Gen X'ers can carry forward that challenging approach to good effect when searching for the best possible manner of delivering training, but it can equally disrupt efforts to share knowledge.

Millennials are very comfortable with most forms of technology, having grown up around computers, the internet, and social media. Boredom with the speed of data delivery from more traditional methods of teaching are a likely point of friction. On the positive side, Millennials work well together in teams and this can be utilized to help verify understanding and collaborate on training delivery.

Gen Z's are the latest addition to the workforce and it's early days to determine specific traits. However, you can expect technological capabilities ahead of Millennials and in particular a preference for smartphone app, podcast and social media-delivered resources.

## Sources of training content and support

Create content for training that offers:

- Face-to-face Q&A in groups and one-to-one;
- Webinar with show notes and online test;
- Pre-recorded video or podcast;
- Group session reviews of training a couple of weeks after original session;
- Set homework; and
- Hand-out notes to support training.

## SWOT analysis – Strengths, Weaknesses, Opportunities, Threats

| Training | Baby Boomers | Gen X | Gen Y (Millennial) | Gen Z |
|---|---|---|---|---|
| Strengths | Written content, lectures | Adaptable to various methods of delivery | Comfortable with online delivery, adept at learning in this mode | Can very quickly absorb data online, adept at using apps |
| Weaknesses | Webinars, online tests | Can become agitated and disruptive if there's a problem | Less comfortable with "talk and chalk" style of delivery | Easily distracted and may lose focus |

| | | | | |
|---|---|---|---|---|
| **Opportunities** | Develop skills with online delivery | Provide plenty of advance notice of training and channels to deliver feedback | Develop skills outside of online to ensure they are not missing out on essential learning | Demonstrate their learning preferences, make them self-aware |
| **Threats** | Technophobic tendency in some BB's | Impact on colleagues when vocalizing concerns | A refusal to adopt other methods of training considering them "outdated" | A single minded approach to the latest methods of delivery |

## Cascading

Often the opportunity will present itself to attend a seminar delivered by a leading authority in a team's area of interest, such as divorce, IP, sports contracts etc. Whatever the topic, it can be difficult if not impractical to organize for the entire department to make the trip.

In such circumstances, those attending should have the objective of securing the key takeaways for their colleagues.

This is a common approach for more informal internal training sessions where learning can be cascaded to others. The downside of such an approach can be the variance in capability of those tasked with cascading. In such cases the prospect of boring Brad or shy Sharon delivering can lead to poor attendance and limited knowledge transfer and an overall loss of value from investing in the original event.

To overcome the above difficulties a range of options may be considered to not only make the most of the opportunity but also tap into those generational preferences to improve your chances of effectively delivering the key messages.

1. Consider having the notes taken by the attendee written up in a common firm-approved format, setting out the subject, overview, context of the seminar and highlighting the key takeaway points along with any actions that should be taken in light of the new information. These should be prepared in PDF format for ease of access from your intranet and/or printed out for those who would prefer to read a hard copy;

2. Have the notes set into a slide presentation and brief the firm's training team (if you have the resource) to deliver the content with the attendee present to take questions;
3. If the attendee is confident and an effective presenter, they should be encouraged to deliver their own training; and
4. Record the internal training on video via smartphone and have it available on the intranet for those who couldn't attend or for new joiners arriving after the original sessions were delivered.

The above are suggestions for freshening up and formalizing cascading sessions. If presenting is an issue for a number of your attorneys and other members of staff it would be worth investing in regular, at least annual, presentation skills training. It is, however, worth stressing that not everyone is comfortable with making a presentation, and many actually loathe such public examinations of their skills. It would therefore be counter-productive to force anxious employees into situations they are uncomfortable with, unless of course it forms a key part of their role. In such circumstances you would need an entirely different approach in evaluating suitability for the role.

## Knowledge gaps

When starting out in your career it's easy to draw on the qualifications recently taken as a platform of knowledge, but expectations based on your experience will not be high. It's therefore a given that you'll have large knowledge gaps and over time you'll fill those with a combination of experience on the job and further training.

With BB's, Gen X, and Millennials, the expectation will be that those gaps are mostly filled and apart from keeping abreast of changes in law, environment and market trends, you will be considered to have a rounded base of qualification, experience and knowledge gained through continual development.

In the real world, of course, things are not quite so straightforward. It is not a natural human condition to look at ourselves critically and examine our own shortcomings so as to better understand where we may improve.

The older we are, the harder it is to undertake such a "self-audit" as the generally-held perception of someone in a senior position or with so many years in a similar role is that they must be an expert. The role of a solicitor/attorney is one that demands knowledge and the confidence it instils in clients. The downside to this is the danger of assumptions and the need to exaggerate our strengths and deny any weaknesses.

In running a successful law firm, you should encourage your staff to be open and honest with regards to their needs for training and support. Presentation skills are an excellent example of a life skill many simply fail to gain, mostly through rational and irrational fears of failure.

A skills audit should form part of your regular appraisal process and be undertaken in a sympathetic and positive manner. It is not a witch-hunt, nor something to be feared, but rather embraced. By encouraging all staff, whatever level, to be open about their needs and being aware of potential shortcomings by noting manager and client feedback, you can begin to develop personal development plans to fill any noticeable knowledge or skills gaps.

### Further qualifications

Staying curious and keeping our minds active throughout our careers is a positive mindset and one that should be encouraged in firms. For many Gen X and Baby Boomers, their last formal training will have been several decades ago.

An example from my own experience as a consultant is noting the increasing level of anxiety-related illness within the workplace. Confident that my clients had undertaken all possible steps to reduce anything but the normal and expected stresses of work, I took a look at trends and data within the sector and other industries. My fears were confirmed, this was indeed a common experience within the modern workplace and in particular appeared to impact Millennials and Gen Z's.

The challenge here was to find a way to support my clients and their staff but not in a way that would make them feel embarrassed. Mental health issues still carry an unwarranted stigma, so a subtle approach was required. My response was to enroll on a cognitive behavioral therapy (CBT) practitioner course so as to better understand the causes of anxiety and appropriate suggestions to help employees. The skills and knowledge gained from the course helped me offer better qualified first level support and, where necessary, signpost to additional professional help. As a result of initial success, training to a wider group of senior managers was recommended and adopted.

This highlights the fact that the answer to further qualification is not always straightforward, but it also demonstrates how we need to adapt to our circumstances.

With the above example in mind, it's worth considering the future of your firm and which skills you believe your practitioners, support staff, and executive managers will need, to maintain the success of the business and engender a positive, supportive, and professional culture.

# Chapter 4: Client and colleague communication

### Communication preferences

Your firm will have systems and processes embedded within the organization that shape the way you interact both internally and externally. Historically, pre-1990s, telephone and written communication via formal letters and reports would be the main method of communication, supported in the late 1980s by fax for more urgent messages.

As the internet began to emerge as the pre-eminent technology for presenting businesses with an effective communication tool – which had already been around for two decades – email found itself at the heart of connecting colleagues and clients.

As digital moved through the noughties to the present day we've seen an emergence of app-based communication platforms, such as Facebook and Facebook Messenger, LinkedIn, Twitter, Instagram, WhatsApp and WeChat to name a few of the more popular varieties. In addition to the app explosion, internal communication options are also plentiful, with any variation on the traditional email via intranet chat functions, facetime, cell/SMS text, Google Mail, and so on.

But where does that leave us when we consider the generational spectrum and most likely "go to" method to reach out to co-workers or our clients?

It won't surprise you to learn that the tendencies follow the timelines. Human nature is nothing if not predictable when it comes to change, we just don't like it. Not to say there aren't those who readily embrace the latest, brightest new option, but those early adopters tend to be in the minority.

Below is a breakdown of generational preferences by communication type and connection. There are always exceptions and not everyone follows the rule; however, it is worth considering that the generations will have their strengths and weaknesses with each tool given their frequency and comfort of use.

## Lawyer communication preferences

1–5 (1 = most preferred)

| | Baby Boomers | Gen X | Gen Y (Millennial) | Gen Z |
|---|---|---|---|---|
| | INTERNAL | | | |
| Meeting | 1 | 2 | 4 | 4 |
| Memo (hard copy) | 2 | 3 | 5 | 5 |
| Phone call | 1 | 1 | 3 | 4 |
| Email | 3 | 1 | 2 | 3 |
| Intranet | 4 | 2 | 2 | 2 |
| Text message | 4 | 2 | 1 | 2 |
| FB/WhatsApp Messaging app | 5 | 4 | 1 | 1 |
| Twitter | 5 | 4 | 2 | 2 |
| LinkedIn | 5 | 3 | 3 | 2 |
| Video/ Skype/ Facetime | 5 | 4 | 2 | 1 |

| | Baby Boomers | Gen X | Gen Y (Millennial) | Gen Z |
|---|---|---|---|---|
| | | EXTERNAL | | |
| Meeting | 1 | 2 | 3 | 4 |
| Letter | 1 | 2 | 5 | 5 |
| Phone call | 1 | 2 | 3 | 4 |
| Email | 2 | 1 | 2 | 3 |
| Via an assistant | 2 | 3 | 5 | 5 |
| Text message | 4 | 3 | 2 | 2 |
| FB/WhatsApp Messaging app | 5 | 4 | 1 | 1 |
| Twitter | 5 | 5 | 2 | 3 |
| LinkedIn | 5 | 4 | 3 | 3 |
| Video/ Skype/ Facetime | 5 | 3 | 2 | 1 |

It's not rocket science to suggest older generations prefer more traditional methods of communication, but surprisingly, when it comes to organizing our approach as a business, we take little if any regard for such bias.

**Case example**

A large firm undertakes a communication audit and determines it is too far behind the curve and needs to upgrade its systems to keep up with competitors. The newly appointed Millennial managing partner is enthused by the presentations of case management systems and intranets that seamlessly link to smartphone accessible apps. After a brief beauty parade of market leading applications, a decision is made, and the investment is authorized by the executive board.

Fast forward six months post launch. The Baby Boomer support staff are very unhappy and wish to turn back to the old system as they no longer feel they can access details of what is happening in the firm. Baby Boomer attorneys are frustrated that they weren't given enough training before launch and now struggle with the new billing process, complaining that clients are getting frustrated with the lack of effective communication.

Generation X mostly accepted that change was inevitable, but a small, vocal group have taken to private social media groups to voice their frustrations. Their concerns are similar to their BB colleagues but there is also an overriding anxiety relating to the choice of supplier and the consequential issue of an overstated return on investment.

Millennials were the most enthusiastic about the changes and have adapted best, happy to see the investment in new technology. They can see that the network is far quicker, and with better Wi-Fi connectivity throughout the offices they can use video conferencing on smartphones, which they had asked for. On the downside, the community-minded Millennials are aware of the disquiet with others and concerned that the changes have not been best implemented. They are therefore less visibly supportive than they may possibly wish to be, so as not to cause issue with their unhappy colleagues.

Gen Z are new in post and mostly in a "probation" mode, which equates to head down, assessing the lie of the land before making any moves. Privately, a number of new joiners are messaging each other, casting doubt over their choice of firm given the poor atmosphere and overall morale within the business.

The above case study demonstrates how the best of intentions and financial investment in the future security of a business can be disrupted by a few key points of irritation localized to individual learning styles and preferences.

To resolve the situation, the managing partner needs to consult with the staff and seek to address concerns. The first step in resolving conflict is to allow their anger to be vented, although that frustration should be encouraged to be shared in a constructive and impersonal manner.

Taking notes, the next step is to ensure expectations are managed. There is little point in promising to fix every issue if the complaint is either irrational or completely counter to a logical strategy. The challenge then is to find a common point of agreement and work to bring the abstainers onboard.

The feedback may also raise questions over project launch and implementation, which reflects on the failings of the supplier. Here a conversation will need to be had to assess the opportunity of revisiting the training, assessing the knowledge gaps and scheduling updates to ensure sufficient information and time is given to those who are expressing difficulties.

Thinking of the wide spectrum of generational diversity, there may be an opportunity to offer choices and rather than direct staff to a pre-determined method of compliance, use the skills they have to make the system work for them.

In each and every IT upgrade I've managed – and there have been dozens – such issues are always raised. Over time you become familiar with the pattern and learn to head off any such stress point before it has a chance to upset the implementation. Without exception, projects succeed because of the flexibility and drive of those at the sharp end of implementation. Having "super users" who are internal experts within each section of the practice can save both time in lost productivity and costs in scheduling further training.

### Client care and handling complaints

During the management of a matter your attorneys will follow the protocols set down by the firm and ensure all compliance measures are adhered to. The critical point of ensuring satisfaction with that client, be they a retired couple looking to update their affairs or the CEO of a billion-dollar concern making yet another deal, is managing expectations.

If the brief from the client, in person, suggests the work will become far more complicated than the initial phone call or email suggests, you'll need to let them know fee estimates will need to increase as a result.

In addition, many cases bring with them a considerable level of stress. If the approach you have adopted for communicating with your clients is a choice they are not comfortable with, and not one of their preferred options, it can add fuel to any potential conflict or dispute with their matter.

A Millennial client who receives only written communication in letter form will be frustrated at the lack of immediacy and accessibility of their law firm, regardless of the quality of work undertaken. Equally, an older client in their late 70s (the Silent Generation) would be potentially confused and unable to engage if the firm is insistent on using messaging apps to update on progress.

There is clear merit in adopting an approach to suit the client, however much this may be at odds with the preferences of the lawyer handling the case.

Understanding generational preferences should be a regular feature of the firm's training and development program, specifically those sessions relating to client care. Potential issues have a far greater chance of being managed at an early juncture by adopting a client communication strategy that suits personal preferences.

The recommendation is for your firm to undertake an audit of its client base to identify the age spectrum of personal and commercial customers. The purpose of this exercise is to better understand the preferences of those clients related to their typical age analysis.

Using the communication preferences below, highlight which activity your firm predominantly uses by making the field content bold. In the example shown we see that this firm's preferred communication method is telephone.

## Client communication preferences

1–5 (1 = most preferred)

*Firm's preferred communication method marked in bold.*

| | Silent Gen | Baby Boomers | Gen X | Gen Y (Millennial) | Gen Z |
|---|---|---|---|---|---|
| Meeting | 1 | 1 | 2 | 3 | 4 |
| Letter | 1 | 1 | 2 | 5 | 5 |
| Phone call | **2** | **1** | **2** | **3** | **4** |
| Email | 3 | 2 | 1 | 2 | 3 |
| Text message | 5 | 4 | 3 | 2 | 2 |

| | | | | | |
|---|---|---|---|---|---|
| FB/WhatsApp Messaging app | 5 | 5 | 4 | 1 | 1 |
| Twitter | 5 | 5 | 5 | 2 | 3 |
| LinkedIn | 5 | 5 | 4 | 3 | 3 |
| Video/ Skype/ Facetime | 5 | 5 | 3 | 2 | 1 |

The most accurate approach, if resources permit, would be to undertake your own survey or revisit any recent research that identifies communication preferences and cross-reference the age profile from your database.

## Handling complaints

If you are in receipt of a formal complaint it will trigger your complaints policy and the process the partnership has agreed to follow. Whilst the general approach – such as time to submit your initial and final response – should be consistent, the style and manner of communication could be adapted to suit the generation.

The key should be to ensure your response is both received and understood in a timely fashion.

Silent Generation and Baby Boomers will, as a general rule, be less reluctant to complain than Generation X and Millennials. The older generations' threshold for acceptable service can be lower as a result of an inherent deference toward the professional services. This is an historic pedestal placement for lawyers who were regarded as pillars of the community. The media has over the years eroded this status somewhat, although it will still hold, predominantly with the older generation.

Younger clients – Gen X, Millennials and Z's – will not be so deferential and whilst appreciating the need for legal professionals will often view accessing services and fees as a necessary pain to undergo. It's not unusual for these confident, tech savvy clients to undertake a level of research before instructing and have established their own parameters of acceptable service before the lawyer has had an opportunity to assert theirs.

Delays and unexpected timescales are one of the primary points of concern, with costs not far behind. Increasingly, lawyers are also being challenged by clients on points of law too, as a direct result of Googling their situation.

These factors can be managed in a positive manner if the firm accepts the above as the reality of the current working life of a lawyer.

Most Gen X and Millennial attorneys will understand and relate to this position; however, Baby Boomer lawyers may become affronted by the "impudence of youth" and this in itself can create a dysfunctional relationship, resulting in a complaint.

Regardless of the generation of the professional, it makes good sense to stay aware of client trends and ensure any grumbles or feedback that don't make their way to a formal complaint are captured and shared. What might be a slight annoyance for a client today could become the factor that generates a complaint in future. By taking a dynamic approach to complaint handling and regularly assessing performance, firms can develop and improve client communications, making it far less likely to generate negative responses.

## Business development

How to generate a greater level of fee income is one of the most frequently posed questions by law firm partners and department heads across the globe. No sooner has a firm devised a cunning strategy and started to see returns, an event or trend will emerge that alters the impact of the strategy and demands a new approach. Our world is moving ever faster, driven by digital innovations and industry disruptors creating an environment of constant change. It's tough out there and we need to grab any advantage we can to hold what we have and profitably grow our businesses.

The generational approach to business development is very simple and effective, yet in my experience very few firms have adopted it.

## Existing clients

We have already mentioned the importance of an audit to establish a better rapport with our existing clients and help refine our communication strategy during matter management. This audit can also serve to inform our thinking when we consider that oft spoken but rarely well executed initiative of cross-selling.

Those clients who have already instructed your firm are the very best opportunities for marketing additional services, but this should not be an excuse to "dumb down" the approach and assume it will be easy to sell in to them.

There are subtle and obvious differences in how different generations purchase goods or services and an awareness of these will go a long way in supporting your efforts and turning a mediocre campaign into a profitable success.

## Lifecycle

Whether a Millennial corporate CEO, or Silent Generation retired couple, there are life events for each age group that will shape their thinking and priorities.

1. **Older Silent Generation** clients will be looking for peace of mind, security, legacy and trust that the job will be completed thoroughly. They will look for a firm with a good reputation and longevity with lawyers that match their expectations.
2. **Baby Boomers** will also be looking to a period where they won't have a salaried income. This also offers freedom to explore new opportunities, but they will want the satisfaction that their affairs are in order with a level of financial security. They too will be keen to appoint or re-appoint a lawyer who they can see has experience and can empathize with their situation.
3. **Generation X** and younger BB's can face the uncomfortable position of supporting both children who may have student debts and are unable to move into their own property, and parents who may have health issues and associated financial difficulties. In their careers they will be established and close to their peak earning potential. Those older Gen X'ers will be looking at retiring within the next ten years whilst the younger X'ers should be trying to build their pension fund. Time-poor, these clients can present a challenge, but if your approach meets their needs, they can prove loyal advocates.
4. **Millennials** still seeing their careers as a means to an end are more driven by life experience than work. This is not to suggest Millennials are not ambitious or capable of creating successful careers and businesses, but they bring a refreshingly different attitude. This generation will place priority on charity and community and will want to see their ethics reflected in the businesses they engage with.
5. **Generation Z**. The new kids on the block may not be appointing lawyers that often but when they do they will likely follow a Millennial lead with regards to charitable interests. The environment

and specifically climate change will be a major influence on their thinking and as a consequence environmentally-responsible businesses will score highly.

The Deloitte Millennial Survey 2019 highlighted a number of factors that this younger generation would take into consideration and seek from their employers. Firms should be minded to consider this fast emerging desire to work in a business that not only provides financial but also moral and ethical security for the employee. For "seek from their employer" also read "seek from the professionals they employ". There is a growing correlation between what consumers want from their suppliers and what they expect from their working environment, and this can tie back to the overall culture of your firm.

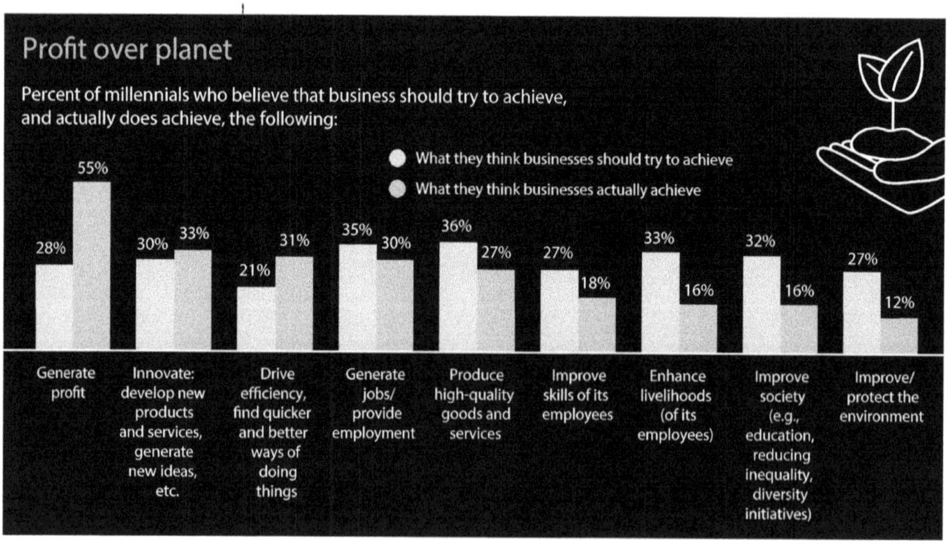


*Figure 1: Business is still out of step with Millennials' priorities. Source: Deloitte Global Millennial Survey 2019 deloitte.com/millennialsurvey*

# Chapter 5: Managing

## Motivation

The often-heard phrase, "Staff leave their manager, they don't leave the company" is so very true. Think back to your own experiences, good and bad, and the impact an effective manager can have on your outlook.

One of the best managers I had the good fortune to work for was a woman called Jackie who headed up the marketing function of a global travel company. That was my second role at the company and my first experience was far less positive.

I secured the new job in marketing following a rather unfortunate experience with another manager who certainly lacked the art of motivation. Once struggling to find a suitable flaw to pull me down, he sneered that in his opinion, "You walk across the department too slowly..." which was nonsense given the work I was undertaking and the general high pace we all operated at. I would also add that I was 19 at the time.

Having moved some distance and left home to take the new job, I was determined to make my way in the company, despite the negativity of someone who clearly objected to any young, ambitious and potentially capable employees. I say potential as he singularly failed to test or encourage me or any of my colleagues, content instead to keep his staff down, feeling threatened for the security of their jobs. This power play simply didn't work on me as my immediate response, following the review, was to spend a large proportion of my salary on a new suit, shirt, tie and shoes, which by all accounts completely threw the manager into fury, believing I had a series of interviews lined up.

My second manager actually motivated her staff. Jackie cared about her team, developed a strong collaborative approach to work, encouraged openness and admission of mistakes so lessons could be learnt. I spent the next ten years with this company and in the process took my Masters in Marketing, inspired by that excellent manager.

What does the above example show us of generational interplay? I am Generation X and the two managers in question were both Baby

Boomers, albeit late in that generation so less than ten years older than me.

Despite the fact that many years have passed, the same issues and opportunities continue to present themselves. As senior managers or CEOs of firms, we must not allow poor managers to deliver negative impressions upon the impressionable and instead promote the best practice of the good manager running productive and motivated teams.

Training can be critical here and, regardless of generation, no one should be immune from learning how to improve their managerial skills.

The most common mistake witnessed within law firm management is the promotion of a capable practitioner to a role where they are expected to manage people. There is little logic in making such a decision, yet influencing the day-to-day activities and performance of others is seen as an easy way to "reward" a lawyer who has proven themselves in their work.

The key should be to identify their skills first and their personality make-up to determine if they would indeed suit such responsibility. There are any number of methods to show progression without, as they often view it, "dumping" staff management on them.

Good bosses actively seek out opportunities to nurture and bring on talent within a practice. For the longer-term success of your business it could be worth making such skills or potential a high priority when recruiting.

## Targets, aka "what good looks like"

Before we can effectively motivate staff, we need to set out their defined goals as applicable to their role. An attorney may be given a fee income target but also a metric for delivering a level of client satisfaction as measured by post-matter feedback. They may also be given encouragement to participate in other role-specific projects and potentially achieve a training or qualification goal.

The specific targets will vary depending on role, seniority, and the overall needs of the business but no one should be engaged without knowing a very basic rule – the need to know "what good looks like", as far as their job is concerned, so they can appreciate the expectations of the firm and work to achieve those outcomes. If you don't set such parameters, you can hardly criticize a member of your team for not meeting your privately held expectations.

### Baby Boomers

Whilst the more mature members of your firm may have miles on the clock, don't assume that they'll not need to be given a target or have it contextualized. As a consequence of their years of experience they will actually expect such communications and should actively welcome the structure such objective-setting provides.

### Generation X

Although often fiercely independent, the X'ers still need to know their expected destination so they can navigate their own path to succeed. Once the map is laid out, they will be happy driving toward the goal under their own steam and won't need too much direction from back seat managers. The worst thing you can do for most staff is micromanage them toward their targets, but if you want to see fireworks, try that with a Gen X! One way to stay in touch with their journey is to suggest a series of milestones to reach along the way and provide opportunities for catch-ups to review these.

### Millennials

Unlike X, this is mostly a generation of team players and collaborators. They may require greater input in goal-setting to help them contextualize the target with their own career path and expectations aligned with that of the firm. This shouldn't be ignored from the older generations but may require more time, notably with younger Millennials.

Having set themselves targets, the Millennial will look for reassurance that their approach is working and here recognition for achievements and early feedback would be welcome. As with X'ers it may prove beneficial to have a series of small goals to reach, leading to their overall target.

### Gen Z

We should pause before making a sweeping assumption and linking the Z's with Millennials, as it's still early days. The best approach is to ensure goal-setting is consistent with other members of staff and learn their preferences and performance levels by working to a regular program of reviews. Note this is not a license to micromanage but simply a recommendation to check in and assess progress versus goals.

## Goal-setting tips

Whichever generation you're setting goals for, you should consider engaging with them to help agree the specific target rather than have strict criteria imposed on them. Being part of the process is in itself a motivational factor and can help create stronger momentum toward meeting objectives.

Individual goals should also be aligned to those of the firm as a whole and specific department targets.

Utilizing SMART objectives helps avoid the trap of creating purely aspirational, vague wish lists. The SMART objective is one that is:

- Specific;
- Measurable;
- Achievable;
- Realistic; and
- Time-scaled.

## Projects, teamwork and collaboration

Most firms experience situations where multiple disciplines find themselves working together on a common case, be that a legal team or a mixture of legal and support staff.

Millennials are tagged as a collaborative generation, which is of course not true for each and every member of that age cohort, but in general terms they have learnt to work together and as a network, helped by their engagement and capabilities with technology.

Older generations are of course not incapable of teamworking, although it is true to say that Generation X has been tagged more than once as the "independent" working generation. As one myself I accept this, but also would add that most of us have adapted and now enjoy working as part of a team.

Baby Boomers can often assume they will be the "go to" lead or head of team. Whilst that may be the correct choice, it should not be an automatic decision based purely on age and respect. BB's have experience that can be essential input to a successful project, but it does not make them the natural leader choice.

Better to let the team work on the problem/scenario, set an agreed objective and task matrix for those participating, and look at the skillset of the team members. If there's one natural leader you often find they are democratically selected. If, however, you have a rather competitive team who are more akin to working like groups in the TV show "The Apprentice" you may need to intervene to make the selection and keep a watchful eye on progress.

Politics are a very real factor in our working environment, and overcoming negative team play must be a priority to afford the greatest opportunity of success.

You can start the team off with a task to agree their rules of engagement – the do's and don'ts. Often very bright and capable contributors are not permitted a voice by the louder, more aggressive, but less productive, members of a team.

This is where a simple set of team rules can help articulate the protocols for reaching decisions and within the election of an agreed team leader.

If it is possible to create teams across the generations, it can prove not only highly successful but a genuinely enlightening process for young and older members who previously held stereotypical views of their team members.

## Problem solving and teamwork

Each generation will face its own set of challenges, both within their career and personally. How they approach their issues and opportunities is shaped by a multitude of factors, which could fill several volumes of psychometric analysis.

As with building teams, firms have engaged this psychometric science to help recruit and appoint teams and to solve certain specific business problems and/or seize target opportunities.

Two of the most popular analysis tools are Myers-Briggs and Belbin.

The Myers-Briggs type indicator is designed to help identify an individual's personality type, strengths, and preferences. The creators of this analysis tool were Isabel Myers and Katherine Briggs, who based their work on Carl Jung's theory of personality types. They created 16 personality types, which have subsequently been assigned to employees across the world.

Belbin's team roles are used to identify an employee's behavioral strengths and weaknesses in the firm, the theory being that Belbin can provide a common language for managers to ensure that individuals and teams communicate and work together effectively.

These can be useful tools for identifying the team's working preferences, revealing strengths and weaknesses for individuals. However, it should not be taken as a definitive piece of analysis with the results assigned to the subject for their entire career. As we mature, we change our outlook and gain skills and experience that shape our thinking.

## Flexible working

Each generation brings a work ethic influenced by their environment, education, parents, peers and previous managers. However, they may not all have experience of the advantages and opportunities of flexible working.

Those responsible for setting such policies may be wary of introducing initiatives such as working from home or flexible hours, but they are increasingly being successfully adopted by businesses across many sectors.

If you have a controlling, strict and traditional culture within a firm it can stifle creative thinking and at a basic level be an uncomfortable place to work, leading to added stress and days off, and ultimately high churn with the knock-on effect of recruiting.

Baby Boomers and Generation X members of the firm may need the most persuasion about the benefits of offering staff a flexible working environment. Looking at the other side of the coin, there is also a realistic and increasing risk to the business in refusing to consider flexible working. Retaining a traditional working hours approach, aligned to strict billable hour targets, might deter talent, especially if it is a known culture trait of your firm. Candidates may prefer a more open, trusting employer and existing staff will see the struggle to recruit high level candidates as a negative pointer to the future of the business.

Below are a few simple flexible working initiatives that can help engender trust and loyalty. Rather than being abused by staff, it has been evidenced by those using these employee-friendly approaches that they deliver greater productivity.

**Working from home**

Offices are often open plan and can prove something of a distraction when it comes to drafting important contracts or studying case notes. This may not work for all roles but when deadlines are approaching and a determined productive effort required, an opportunity to work away from the office in the comfort of your own home can be a perfect solution. To guard against abuse, the trade-off should be in having a contact number to get hold of the employee in an emergency and naturally, output should be reviewed to ensure the work is being done. Perhaps start by offering a day or two per month and allow the staff member to decide when they take it.

You can also look at partial home working days. This would be where a staff member would start the day at home and be in the office for a meeting later that afternoon, perhaps preparing for that meeting during the home working period. Depending on the role and demands, this could be part of the working schedule, although it would be advisable to insist on regular contact at any given time to avoid any potential issues when trying to get in touch.

### Flexi-time

Systems can be used to implement a form of flexi-time that literally sees employees clock in and out so their time can be monitored and any time over their contracted hours can be taken as additional time off above permitted holidays. Such systems can provide useful data for HR but can be open to abuse or work against a business where employees in teams are not coordinating their hours or time off.

As a general rule, flexi-time works well in the professional service sector. Most firms will have core hours to cover and as long as those hours are met, employees could be offered flexibility in their daily start and end time. For example, Jeff could start at 7am and leave at 3pm. Tanya could start later, say 10am but leave at 6pm. This flexibility can be of particular assistance to staff with school-age children or with child-care needs.

To implement flexi-time it would be advisable to have staff state their preferred working day start and end point and suggest they stick to those hours to provide a level of consistency and certainty when they are on site. It's also important to stress that departments provide full cover and staff coordinate and agree between themselves how best to achieve that goal.

### Job sharing

The business may have a clear need for a full-time post; however, that may be met by two part-time workers. This can work well in administrative positions and as long as client care is to the fore, attorneys too can job share. Lawyers sharing jobs is not as common as other positions but with the trend toward family-friendly policies and older lawyers wanting to remain at work, it is becoming increasingly popular. You could well see a Millennial parent and a semi-retired Baby Boomer working the same position at different ends of the day; one AM, the other PM, or one working three days and the other two.

### Remote working

With digital technology it is possible for many professional service practitioners to meet KPIs (Key Performance Indicators), without fulfilling the nine-to-five office appearance. The rising costs of commuting for staff and impact on the climate, office rent and the associated investment in office furniture and equipment can be reduced by enabling a remote workforce. There are certain firms who are almost entirely "virtual" in that the workforce is home-based and travels to meet clients at their location. The advantage of such an arrangement is the significant flexibility for employees as well as the significant savings in real estate, which can make for a very profitable operation.

### Technology and management

We've mentioned systems and digital advancements, but one area that we have yet to address is that of coordinating systems and applications. This is essential to ensure any staff who are working away from an office can communicate to those in the office effectively – and vice versa. The typical software applications used for such activities are intranets. A system that can provide ready, remote access from PC, smartphone or tablet to information necessary for the employee to stay connected and undertake their role is essential.

Millennials and Gen Z's will be familiar with platforms that provide access to multiple applications and the associated technology, such as voice recognition transcription or digital dictation. Most current case management and accounts packages offer iOS or Android application varieties so as to enable updates and accessibility "on the move" or simply away from the office.

Many Baby Boomers and for that matter Gen X's can be reluctant to adopt new methods of working, especially if linked to new technology. That's not to say they are all technophobes; it is simply human nature to want a straightforward, understood and relatively simple way of working. These generations have lived through a significant amount of technological change already so the recommendation would be to provide a generous element of your IT budget on training and support for staff.

### Time management and flexible working

If the firm has adopted flexible working it is worth taking the opportunity to refresh all staff, without patronizing them, on the key principles of time management. Many workers need the discipline of a work environment to function in "work mode". If that is removed, they may be tempted to procrastinate and be distracted by the many other things they could find to do other than work!

This often won't be a conscious decision to waste company time but the discipline to work from home is one that needs to be developed, and depending on the environment they live in, can be harder for some than others.

## Time management tips for staff – working from home

1. Be professional. Whilst you might not need the "power suit" on the days where you're not meeting clients or heading into the office, you should make an effort. Being in pajamas or a robe all day can make you feel as though you're skipping work, not just working differently;
2. Have a clear goal – you should have a set list of actions and realistic goals to achieve for each day. By working through the list, you gain a sense of achievement and confidence. Get into the habit of keeping the lists logged; it will support any questions over productivity away from the office;
3. Don't be tempted to watch TV or that Netflix box set on your laptop. Equally, don't get lost in a meander through Google. Avoid such distractions;
4. Try and get ALL domestic chores done out of work hours and don't be drawn into "I could just mow the lawn, wash the car, iron those clothes". Procrastination is all too easy when you're not being watched;
5. To overcome the tempting thoughts to do anything but work, set yourself small rewards for achieving certain milestones in your day;
6. Take breaks but make them proper breaks, not opportunities to revert to any of the time-wasting distractions you might be tempted by;
7. Make time for a proper lunch break just as if you were in the office and popping out with colleagues;
8. Don't become too immersed in work. Whilst many think "working from home" is code for a sneaky day relaxing, the truth can be that staff can over-compensate for the added flexibility and end up heading into workaholic territory. Retain a healthy balance;
9. If working on a particularly heavy case, set a timer to ensure that you remain focused on all the tasks you've set yourself to achieve that day;
10. Enjoy the freedom. Enjoy your shortest ever commute to work, allow yourself the opportunity to relax, rather than becoming anxious about the potential isolation of periods working from home;

11. Take time to connect with colleagues, keep yourself "in the loop" and accessible. If the job involves long periods without seeing managers or colleagues, find a reason to reach out; and
12. If you're not asked to provide regular updates on progress, provide supervisors with access to a folder containing your daily schedules and weekly summary. It will demonstrate your organizational skills and openness and build trust in your work within the firm.

## Mentoring

During my career, I have both engaged individuals as my mentor and acted as a mentor to others. I am a strong advocate of using such a relationship to support and help guide individuals through their careers, from day one trainee through to chair of the board. If you identify the right level of mentor it can prove hugely beneficial.

When younger members of staff were once asked at my firm what they thought a mentor looked like, the almost unanimous answer was older, probably grey haired, near retirement or retired and a well-known figure in their industry. Those assumptions may well meet the profile of very capable mentors, but it's by no means a definitive description of those who can offer mentoring support.

One reason for my passion for this subject is borne from my experience running a regional mentoring program. When I took over, this government-funded program was not doing well. I took time to meet with a number of mentees who had most recent experience and the feedback concerning the existing mentors on the program was not good. "He was arrogant", "comes across as knowing it all", "He's never available when I need to speak to him", "Rather patronizing" were a few of the more positive comments.

The problem was caused by the previous organizer of the group who had made a rather calamitous assumption similar to those thoughts of the younger members of my firm – that mentors must be 50+ and predominantly male and be in jobs such as bank manager, solicitor, accountant, or headteacher. These individuals did not understand the principles of mentoring; instead they would launch into coaching their mentees and tell them where they were going wrong, often without fully understanding the mentee's business.

I sacked 11 of the 12 mentors on the original program and began recruiting a new cohort based on a few simple but critical skills:

- Good listeners;
- Personable;
- Nurturing;
- Non-judgmental; and
- Interesting life experience.

Unsurprising to me was the fact that eight of the 11 new recruits were female and the average age fell from 58 to 39. I put all 12 and myself through a mentoring training program and created a set of principles by which we would work for the mentees.

The mentoring program became one of the leading initiatives of its kind in the UK and and (of greater importance to me) delivered dozens of positive working relationships that generated hugely successful, award-winning businesses.

Mentoring is not for everyone but neither is it the domain of an elite grey-haired brigade of "executives" playing at altruism. Mentors can be younger than the mentee, from different countries, sectors, religious backgrounds etc., but they must share a passion for helping people and the desire to see positive outcomes.

The use of mentors in the legal profession can be a true force for good in supporting staff at all stages of their career, but I have often witnessed such activities treated with lip service and not given the true management support needed to be successful. They often fall into that trap of nominating older members of the executive board to become a mentor rather than identifying the most appropriate individuals.

If you are serious about developing or growing your mentoring program, give serious consideration to hiring an external resource to evaluate the personality and capabilities of potential mentors and select a group. Provide the group with the best possible training you can source and offer ongoing access via a trusted forum where any issues and challenges can be shared in confidence without divulging personal details of mentees.

Each generation and member of staff within the firm should be given the opportunity to have a mentor, as it can make a significant impact on morale and boost the positivity of your culture.

## Conflict and discipline

*"Any problem, big or small, within a family, always seems to start with bad communication. Someone isn't listening."*
Emma Thompson

In our careers we will very likely encounter situations where we find ourselves as both the recipient and deliverer of a form of disciplinary. Our experiences can often shape the way we behave in future exchanges of a similar nature, in the same way parenting can influence us into adulthood.

Being a parent is certainly a challenge and any number of self-help books cannot prepare you for the uncommunicative teenager or peer pressured ten-year-old desperate for her first smartphone.

What's that got to do with running a law firm? Actually, quite a lot. It's about communication and generational adaptation. Without effective communication our businesses will simply fail. Without a set of rules by which we set out what we consider to be reasonable and unreasonable behavior, chaos will reign.

In the vast majority of cases a conflict at work is caused by a breakdown of communication.

Here are a few examples:

- Missing a billing target and hiding from the head of department to avoid the inevitable questions because of an irrational fear that they may lose their job;
- Emailing a joke that is in very poor taste;
- Being very loud on the telephone in an open plan office;
- Telling a client that their first meeting is free and then sending them a bill;
- Checking a smartphone multiple times when in a department meeting; and
- Being indiscreet about the details of a client's divorce when chatting at the watercooler.

But what of communication across the generations? How can that create conflict?

Newly-appointed Millennial senior associate, flush from winning a new large client, takes a dislike to the branding of the firm and tells the

Baby Boomer managing partner she thinks it's "old fashioned" and out of touch.

The managing partner, who briefed the original design and had always received very positive feedback, immediately goes on the defensive, asking for the marketing qualification and credentials of the senior associate.

The pointed response annoys the senior associate who now considers the managing partner to be arrogant and too rigid in his thinking.

Taking this scenario and rethinking the approach by the Millennial, would she have had a better response if she'd said:

"You know I'm a big fan of the firm's marketing, it's one of the reasons I joined the firm, but I note a lot of firms are refreshing their look. I think if we built on what we already have but, let's say, gave it a makeover, it could be amazing."

It's a more positive approach, paying deference to the company's history. It doesn't assume that the managing partner will automatically see her point of view and it permits the older partner a chance to offer a balanced opinion rather than finding it necessary to defend a long-held management decision.

There are any number of such conversations taking place throughout firms and, with as many as five generations co-existing, it demands an appreciation of where each is coming from and sufficient emotional intelligence not to light the fuse and damage relationships.

### Reward

When a team delivers a new account, or an individual performs significantly above target, it's only appropriate to consider rewarding their efforts.

Each firm will have a tradition of reward, which can be:

- A celebratory meal hosted by the executive board;
- A gift or voucher;
- Straightforward hard cash, bonus payment;
- Promotion; and/or
- A bottle of expensive wine or champagne.

These gestures would always be welcome – you may think – but amongst young Millennials and Gen Z the sense of community is strong and being singled out isn't always perceived as positively as in the past.

Naturally a promotion or bonus would be welcome, especially if looking to reduce debts or trade up in real estate, but there are subtle signals emanating from the younger generations that "greed is not good" and the preference would be to see something that would benefit more than just one or a small team.

If the team are a cross-generational group then we may have yet another example of a potential conflict.

The advice would be to take soundings before deciding on rewards based on tradition or what has worked before. What appeals to a Baby Boomer or Gen X will not necessarily float the boat of a Millennial or Gen Z.

## Evaluation

Having set goals for all staff, with everyone motivated, energized and clear about their objectives and those of the firm, do you now sit back and expect to see the business take off?

It may well be enough, but more likely there's a risk that no further engagement from senior executives will cause drifting like a sailing boat with no rudder. All generations need to know that someone is in charge, but that doesn't give license for a domineering, directive management style.

Putting systems and processes in place to capture the KPIs of staff and letting them know how their data is being analyzed and reported and discussed will do no harm, as long as it is couched in a positive message.

Better still is the development of self-evaluation and management, which I am seeing a far greater level of. Expected practice management tools can analyze individual, team, and department performance and spew out reams of reports or PDFs to circulate – but that's not always effective. What works is the active engagement of staff in assessing their own performances and teamwork that helps support members who are falling behind.

Support for such efforts can take the form of regular team meetings, but one of the most effective visual aids is a simple whiteboard that can highlight the metrics of the targets and potentially any specific goals of the collective or individuals.

Managed in the right spirit, without a "blame culture" or overt competitive edge that results in intimidation of others, this method can work very well. The senior management team are then free to review the data produced by their self-evaluation as well as the management and dynamics of the group, identifying management talent previously hidden from view.

If staff (and by this I literally refer to ALL members of a team, administrative and legal practitioners) take ownership of the challenge, they are far more likely to find creative ways within their team structure to achieve the target.

If a problem arises within a team and it requires executive intervention, that option should always be available but as last resort rather than the first knee-jerk reaction to anxiety over missing goals.

The collaborative approach works well with Millennials and Gen Z; however, Gen X tend not to be so enthusiastic and Baby Boomers need to know they're not above teamwork and should be encouraged to support less experienced members.

The key to success is ensuring everyone understands and signs up to the overall target and commits to hit their KPIs for the team goal. This is helped by the initiative being driven from the very top of the firm and adopted by everyone. A selective approach will simply not work in the long-term.

# Chapter 6:
# Innovation

When we think of innovation, it is easy to fall into a stereotypical trap that suggests only the younger generations can be truly innovative. These thoughts are driven by the proliferation of technological developments and fears that older workers, managers, and leaders will simply not have the attitude or aptitude to "keep up", let alone proactively participate in the process.

Of course, such narrow thinking is neither helpful nor essentially correct. Who recalls Mark Zuckerberg's infamously ageist comment, "Young people are just smarter". It's the "Digital Native" tag applied to Millennials and Gen Z's that supporters of the Zuckerberg view often turn to.

When we look at the facts, we find quite a refreshing and counter argument for not overlooking the older generation in recruitment, promotion, or leadership roles. Recent research undertaken by Benjamin Jones and Javier Miranda of the US Census Bureau, and MIT's Pierre Azoulay and J. Daniel Kim, found the most successful entrepreneurs are actually middle-aged. The study of 1,700 founders concluded that the average age was 45 and "A 50-year-old founder is 1.8 times more likely to achieve upper-tail growth than a 30-year-old founder".

Whereas younger founders may benefit from their creative thinking and lesser degree of entrenchment in an industry, the exact opposite qualities work to the benefit of their older counterparts.

History can point to a long list of older innovators who created winning businesses when most might be considering retirement, such as David Duffield, who founded software business Workday in 2005 at the age of 65. Workday went public in 2012 and today has a $26.47 billion market cap.

This is just one example of a growing number of older entrepreneurs who marry innovative drive to experience which can provide a winning approach to developing a successful new venture.

However, there is certainly no shortage of Millennial and Gen Z innovators. The energy and adaptability of engaging technology with creative thinking has seen an explosion in business start-ups, with many proving to be global successes, not least Zuckerberg's own modest business born whilst still at university.

Innovation is a mindset and one we should not limit to a specific age group.

## Creativity

Of course, as with innovation, no single generation can claim exclusive rights to creativity. There are those within each age group who have greater creative talent and expression than others, but how those skills are identified and shared is quite different amongst the generations.

Spotting creativity may not seem a high priority for those running a law firm, but it is the creative thinkers who often find the successful solution to that almost impossible problem.

In a more traditional sense, creativity is also seen in the many ways that workers choose to unwind or relax away from their place of work. In a later chapter we look at how this can potentially develop into alternative income generators, career paths, or side hustles.

Providing an opportunity for employees to express creative talents in the workplace has been found to stimulate positive attitudes towards the working environment, allowing hidden talents to earn employees new-found respect.

## Thinking differently

The lateral approach can prove highly profitable, be it the solution to a client problem, a marketing campaign that sparks great engagement, or an operational suggestion that significantly reduces costs for the firm.

Within most organizations exists the creative thinking that can address the above scenarios – the trick is to release these thoughts in a way that encourages rather than stifles. All too often I've witnessed latent talent within a firm side-lined because of factors that proved harder to manage or encourage. What some may see as an "awkward" personality may be the result of a painful shyness or other less easily diagnosed condition. Based on our increasingly better understanding of the way our brains work and personality traits, it's commonly believed that a large number of history's most brilliant minds and innovators were on the autistic spectrum, including Albert Einstein, Barbara McClintock, Steve Jobs, Michelangelo, Emily Dickinson, and Mozart.

There are many more than this; however, given the contribution these six individuals made, it is worth considering within your firm those who may not be a-typical "joiners" in contributing toward the firm's development. They could be just the people you really need to spend time working with. With better knowledge and diagnosis, such conditions are now openly discussed by the younger generations. Those of an older generation, however, may feel a stigma attached to being "branded" with what they may consider to be a condition that could adversely affect their career prospects. Any conversations to stimulate engagement will need to be very sensitively handled and it is recommended professional advice be sought in these circumstances.

Assuming you now have a body of bright and engaged staff happy to participate in your "think tank" how would you go about the process?

- Sparking idea generation – consider having a forum where you have individuals looking at areas they are not directly involved in or ANY function/strategic topic offering a free reign. Attendees should be from diverse backgrounds and levels of the firm;
- Credit where credit is due – you know that moment when your idea is taken by a colleague and presented as their own. Nothing is more demotivating than taking the recognition away from the creative originator. Be sure to have meetings chaired by those who are charged with looking out for such activities and providing the appropriate positivity for those coming up with strong suggestions;
- Free thinking – we've all heard the phrase "No idea is a bad idea" and then witnessed the negative response to a leftfield thought and then been too afraid to take risks. Set rules and ensure participants retain respect for everyone and each suggestion to instill confidence and encourage creative thinking;
- Diversity – as mentioned above, having a group from diverse backgrounds, age, positions, departments, cultures etc. can help in both improving inclusivity and acceptance of colleagues' contributions and the quality of idea filtering;
- Look beyond the business – thinking only of matters inside the firm and of direct influence can be limiting. Innovations in sectors other than legal can be used as case studies to spark thoughts of new applications within the business; and
- Broadcast success – don't overlook the opportunity to let others know within the firm of the think tank's output and projects that result in successful outcomes.

## Adaptation to change

Being in a state ready for action in the face of new information is the aim of most management boards but all too often the day-to-day business of running a busy practice gets in the way of such farsighted planning.

Business continuity planning isn't simply a box ticking exercise for quality accreditation, it can be the difference between serious financial difficulties, survival, and capitalizing on the new situation.

Here it's an opportunity to use those older, more experienced, heads to provide essential input and pass on the benefit of living through challenging circumstances.

### Market conditions

Consider the steps required by firms based in the UK that have been faced with the referendum decision to leave the European Union and "Brexit" – here there has been almost three years to prepare but not a great deal of certainty as to the expected terms of departure. When dealing with clients based in mainland Europe, firms will need to offer reassurance and as clear a path to their future as possible. This is a challenge for most businesses, not just the legal sector, but there exists an opportunity for law firms to offer UK-based commercial clients the best possible advice on preparing for their needs post-Brexit.

### The law

Changes to legislation can affect firms positively or negatively. There is not a great deal that can be done if an income stream is suddenly reduced or lost through a legislative change; however, staying close to political debates, events, and trends that could result in influencing legal affairs must be a priority.

### Personal

Life can throw up any number of challenges and having the strength and ability to deal both physically and mentally can make a huge difference to the individual and those who rely upon them. Supporting initiatives to help in promoting a healthy workforce is one positive step in this effort to establish a firm capable of coping with any situation.

# Chapter 7: Technology

## Timeline of developments

We have covered a number of points on the subject of technology throughout the book, not least in chapter five, but there is no harm in revisiting this increasingly important subject.

In this chapter we will look specifically at the way firms are currently utilizing their technology and how staff are charged with increasing productivity through its effective application.

Before launching into the present office tech, it's helpful to remind ourselves of the journey many of our staff members have taken during their careers. Older Baby Boomers will recall their first days in an office in the mid-1950s, when the office was very much a male domain. Cigarette-, cigar-, and pipe-smoking lawyers making use of the resources available in a typing pool and the only tech other than the typewriter was a Bakelite phone into which secretaries would be given direction to contact a client on the lawyer's behalf.

In the 1960s the workplace began to change from a series of designated offices with secretarial support posted in communal areas to a series of cubicles. Technology hadn't moved very far but one item proved to be a major success, the Xerox copier. The first commercially produced photocopier was the Xerox 914, which produced copies onto sheets 9" by 14". This technology proved a big hit with the legal sector and businesses across the world.

The huge machines often required doors to be removed so they could get into the office. Once in situ they were soon put to work and by 1966 the US was producing 14 billion copies a year. This was a significant uplift in photocopying, given that prior to the launch of the 914, in 1959, the figure was a mere 20 million copies a year (Smithsonian).

The 1970s heralded the arrival of the microprocessor by Intel, which led to the affordability of computers in the business world. Initially their application in the workplace was a single function, such as timecard or attendance processor, rather than the functions we more commonly use them for today.

The 1980s saw the introduction of the PC and technology that I recall being fascinated by when the equipment first arrived in my place of work – the fax machine. Now almost instant transfer of documents was possible, and it made a significant impact on many industries, not least the legal world.

In the 1990s we were handling floppy discs, getting excited about a thing called a "mobile phone" that required a gym-toned physique to carry around, and finding ourselves looking out across the expanse of "open plan" office space.

2000s technology starts to escalate fast with smartphones, social media, digital dictation via apps and a myriad of technologies that capitalized on the internet revolution. We could video conference across the globe and do this courtesy of 3G connectivity.

Blackberry introduced new generations to the ability to email "on the go" via their handset, and when Steve Jobs announced the iPhone in 2007 our lives were changed – and some may say our attention spans lost.

In the 2010s the technological push for greater speeds, bandwidth, and data pushed us into "the cloud", which in turn provided an accessibility option for homeworking and increased reliance on our smartphones. Additionally, laptops and tablets became increasingly popular, further aiding mobility but also "an always available" downside if unchecked.

This quick journey through time provides an indication of the changes older generations have lived through. Certainly the advances in the past 20 years have been staggering and it is no surprise that many struggle to keep up with developments.

## Aptitude and expectation

Here we look at each generation in terms of their tendency to respond to a new practice management system or process involving newly introduced technology. We will assume here that most implementations will be professionally handled by both the IT department and suppliers; however, it's useful to take stock of the potential risks with projects of this nature and in particular the obstacles that may be put in your way.

### Baby Boomers

Having worked through the seismic changes of the past few decades, many BBs are settled with their own levels of technological competence and are often the least enthusiastic when a new system is introduced. They will need to be given plenty of notice and clarity as to the positive outcomes regarding productivity and costs so as to quantify the objectives for such an investment of their time (this may also hold true for Gen X below).

### Generation X

Fiercely independent and not wanting to appear "out of touch", this generation works hard to keep up with developments but is not always as accomplished as they think. Finding the time to delve into the workings of a new system can be trying for those who want to focus on what they consider "productive" time. Of course, tackling and making best use of a new system will help in the long run.

### Millennials

Millennials are very comfortable with most forms of technological innovation as they've grown up in an era of constant "updates" and advancements. This comfort with tech can have a downside – over-confidence. One often witnessed trait of Millennials is something that can often be a real positive, and that is thinking ahead of the problem. Joining the dots within a particularly difficult problem to swiftly arrive at a solution is a skill identified with many Millennial lawyers and support staff. Unfortunately, this ability can on occasion trip them up when conclusions are arrived at that are not correct. To avoid any confusion over methods of implementing the technology it would be advisable to set out the desired approach clearly and check-in post training to ensure adoption has been as expected. Nothing undermines the success of an IT project more than a cohort of Millennials who have taken an alternative approach or, worse, taken against the new system. It is critical that they and all staff are made to feel part of the process long before the launch date.

### Generation Z

New to the work environment, their first encounter with a change in system may prove disruptive. Less comfortable with email, they may not always pick up on important messages relayed in this format. Keep communication varied and fresh, including regular face-to-face engagements. On the upside, Gen Z's can act as very useful test pilots or sense checkers for any proposed "new" system, ensuring the technology is not already out of date. This may sound a rather odd statement given firms generally have IT departments; however, the speed of technological development cannot be underestimated, as the time taken to develop software by specialist legal tech suppliers can run into many years. Having witnessed a couple of close call decisions involving dated software it is worth gathering as much support as you can when considering what is often a hefty long-term investment.

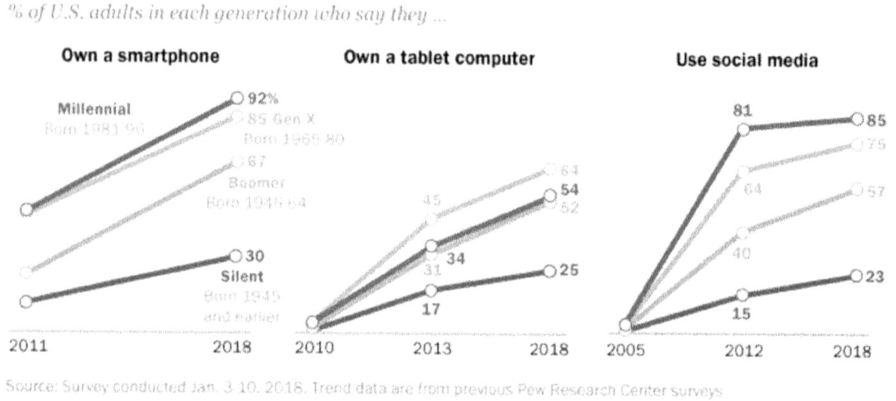


*Figure 1: Technology use by device type and generation. Source: Pew Research Center*

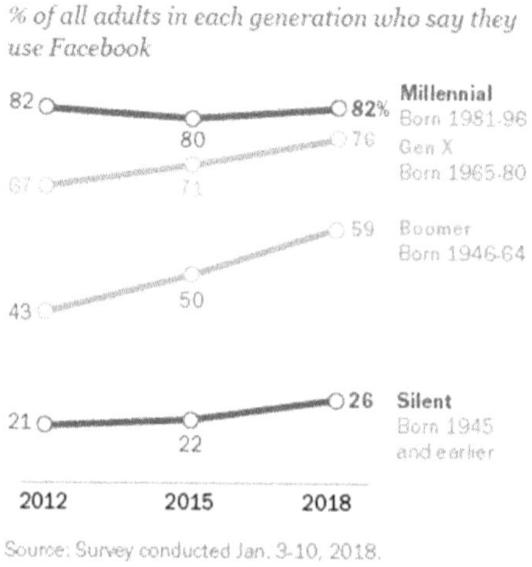


*Figure 2: Generational use of Facebook. Source: Pew Research Center*

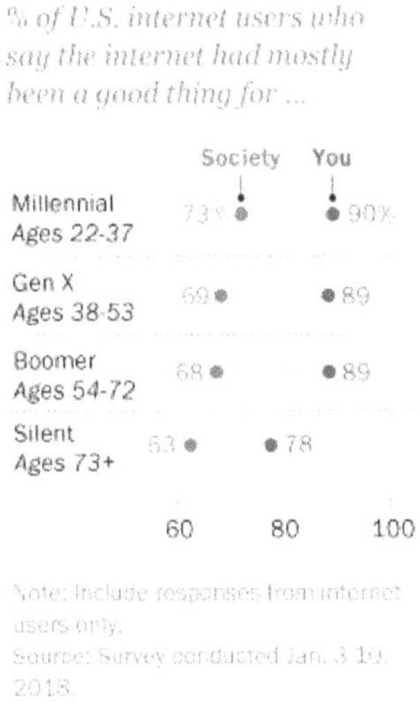


*Figure 3: Older generations are not as positive about the internet as Millennials. Source: Pew Research Center*

## The future

5G technology and the ability to stream and download content will add further weight (in use terms) to our ironically ever slimmer devices. We can expect the increased use of foldable screens, augmented and virtual reality, with holographic outputs.

Of specific interest to the legal sector, blockchain and smart contracts will potentially have far reaching consequences as the power to transact moves toward the consumer rather than reliance upon professional practitioners. In truth, we don't know what the future holds – but the pace of change is not slowing.

Technology is permitting law firms to reconsider the traditional model of running a legal business. Virtual firms, where lawyers are based remotely, often at home, reporting into a lean executive and support hub are now commonplace and are likely to continue to grow in number. The cost of real estate and providing a home for a large office hits the bottom line of most businesses hard. The advantage of the virtual practice is the cost saving and immediate work versus life balances such arrangements can have for lawyers.

# Chapter 8:
# Side hustles and slash careers

## Side hustle

A further consequence of technological advancement is the freedom it has granted those who have entrepreneurial tendencies or a passion for a particular pastime. Those taking on additional income streams are predominantly Millennials and Gen Z who are capitalizing on both their digital skills and trend towards online purchases and need for additional cash to pay bills, including student debt.

A side hustle is simply an additional revenue-generating venture that can exist alongside their main job. The term has grown out of the fast-moving entrepreneurial hotbed of Silicon Valley.

Example side hustles:

- Ride/car sharing;
- Babysitting;
- Dog walking;
- Property letting or development;
- Freelancing;
- Baking;
- Children's party entertainer;
- Personal assistant;
- Fitness coach;
- Yoga/dance/language teacher;
- Laundry services;
- Fashion – vintage clothing, dressmaking, jewelry; and
- Blogger/influencer.

Side-show jobbers have been turbo boosted by technology, which has enabled an almost instant move from idea to action without the previously limiting concerns over set-up costs and risk.

A recent report by Henley Business School (HBS) highlighted the significant growth of such activity and the impact on the economy.

HBS states that these ventures contribute billions of dollars to the economy and are on the rise. The research by HBS indicates a significant percentage of the population undertaking such extra curricular income generation. In the UK, on average, 25 percent of the adult population participates in such activity with the north-east of England being the top region, with 30 percent of adults operating side hustles.

As an employer it would be helpful to know those members of staff who are undertaking such activity. You will of course need to be mindful that, providing their side-hustle is legal and not impacting either their performance or the competitive advantage of your business, you have no automatic right to know what they are doing.

What may be helpful is an inclusive approach that encourages side-hustlers to come forward and benefit from the experience of your organization, which knows they may be on to the next "big idea". As long as there is no direct conflict or loss of focus within their employed role, the supportive mentoring of your in-house side-hustlers will engender greater trust and more likely keep you in the loop with regards to their longer-term ambitions. Any suggestion that their employed position may be in any jeopardy must be very clearly clarified throughout this communication process as it will be an anxiety point for the employee, which may prevent them from coming forward.

We need to accept that we are living in a fast-evolving, uncertain world and employee fears over their future economic position and mid- to long-term employment prospects are sound reasons to seek alternative income streams.

The HBS research identified that more than 50 percent of business leaders admitted they had no policy on side-working, and no process to record and monitor these activities among their workforce.

The majority of bosses were also not expecting any significant increase in the trend over the next five years. This would suggest that there is a generational divide at play with Baby Boomers and Generation X business owners and managers unaware of entrepreneurial activities. Given an average of 25 percent already participating in the practice, those who continue to ignore the trend will be entrenched in traditional nine-to-five workplace-based thinking.

The HBS research highlighted that employees increasingly want to work with businesses that embrace change and that those prepared to support their side-hustling staff will be rewarded with a happier, more fulfilled workforce.

As suggested above, an open dialogue with staff offering support and encouragement rather than fear or restriction will help to engender trust and understanding of the interests of those working in your firm.

From a purely practical perspective, without suggesting this be approached in a heavy handed or "big brother" style, there is a clear need to identify any potential conflicts where, innocently, a member of staff is engaging in indirect or direct competitive activities whilst believing they are not breaching any employment contracts. Often staff are not aware that what they do in their spare time may be subject to restrictions. Education on such do's and don'ts can help prevent future problems.

Whilst staff may not be obliged to share their spare time activities with their employer, an induction session on their obligations would be one way to address the issue. This session could include examples of activities that might breach intellectual property or their terms of employment and offer an open door to any member of staff unsure if their proposed side hustle is indeed a conflict of interest.

## Slash careers

Slash careers, also known as hybrid careers, are similar to side hustles in that the purpose is to maximize income potential but, essentially, they differ in that rather than operate as a separate business, they are defined roles.

The original "Slash" phrase can be traced back to Marci Alboher's 2007 book, *One Person/Many Careers – The Original Guide to the Slash Career.*

This is no passing fad or fancy but an established aspect of today's economy. The US Freelancer Union put the number of workers with multiple roles at 41 percent – quite a significant proportion of the workforce.

The prevalence of slash careers has been in a large part driven by the "gig economy" and business models that relied upon a fluid, freelance workforce that were not "employed" by the main operator. Companies such as Uber and Lyft are often quoted alongside the gig term but many freelancers operate through specialist websites such as Upwork or Fiverr where they will bid for contracts through a structured and trusted platform.

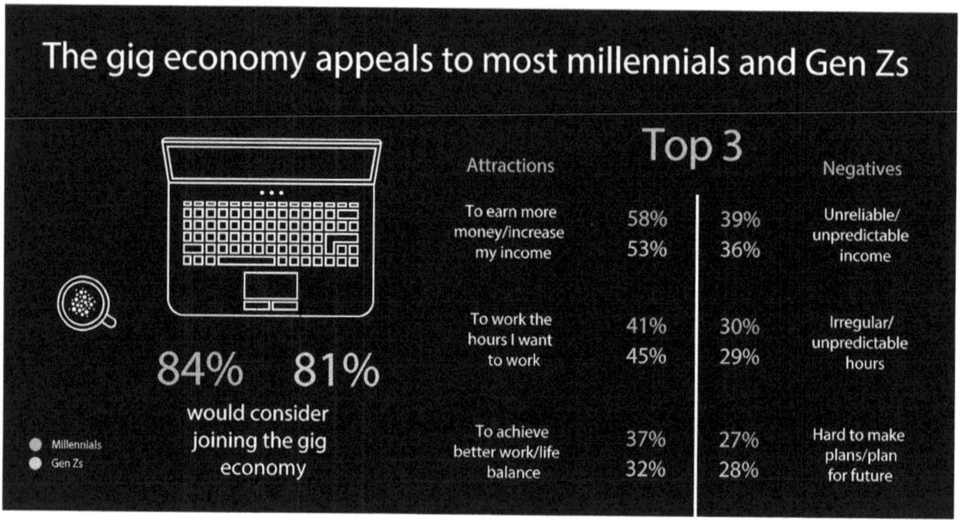


*Figure 1: The gig economy. Source: Deloitte Millennial Survey 2019*

Often, slash careers are linked such as HR with a recruitment professional/career guidance coach/presentation skills trainer.

As with side hustles, those who choose to take on multiple careers tend to be Millennials or Generation Z. Global recessions and continued political and economic uncertainties have driven many to seek the assurance of these multiple income streams, knowing if one were to stop the others would keep them in food and shelter. A basic but very human response to an uncertain future and one often seen in Maslow's hierarchy of needs. When we're threatened, we look to adapt and find ways to survive and thrive. Adopting a multiple career path protects us from a catastrophic loss of income and fear of being supplemented by automation, a consequence of many workers of Baby Boomer and X generations. It's little wonder we now have this multiple career path fast emerging as the norm.

Slash career examples:

- Attorney/photographer;
- Marketing consultant/SEO specialist/social media trainer;
- Events coordinator/wedding planner/baker;
- Architect/graphic designer/environmentalist; and
- Physical education teacher/personal coach/nutritionist.

Lack of awareness of our employees' work commitments outside of the "day job" may seem to traditionalists as the norm, not wanting to become embroiled in personal affairs. The reality is their extra curricular activities could work for or against your firm, and until you enter into a meaningful and positive dialogue with staff you will remain unaware of either the risk or opportunity.

Given the proliferation of both side hustle interests and slash career choices it would be sensible for your firm to adopt a set of appropriate questions when interviewing candidates. Once appointed, your induction process should also accommodate space for a one-to-one communication, relaying the firm's clear position on acceptable behaviors and offering ongoing support for those identified as participating in activities that do not conflict with the interests of the firm.

# Chapter 9:
# Out of office – work/life balance

It is fair to say that each generation brings its own particular strengths and weaknesses to the workplace. To throw a generational spanner in the works, what may be considered a weakness by some can be seen as a strength in others. It's not a clear-cut view.

Your role in managing this diverse group is to ensure you maximize the very best of each generation and in so doing don't overlook areas where they may be at odds with others, or simply struggling due to a misguided conception of what they should be seeking from work and life outside it.

This chapter looks at the various aspects that influence our lives outside of work but are intrinsically linked to the way we act and perform in the workplace. As with all generational traits, they are not exclusive or comprehensive within each age group but give an overview of what you can expect.

## Approach to working life

Baby Boomers have a traditional work ethic, putting in the hours, the appearance of commitment and graft, and more likely to be termed "workaholic". They are likely to frown upon those who don't offer the same commitment as they do or who regularly talk of "work/life balance". On the upside, many BB's were responsible for the technological advances that are now benefiting younger generations. As this generation now nears retirement, they will see the advantages of workplace flexibility offering more leisure time yet still affording periods of work where an income will be valued. There will be increased opportunity to explore leisure time activities as many BB's take semi-retirement/part-time roles, ensuring their employer retains access to their valuable depth of knowledge whilst affording them the opportunity to bring on their successors. Whereas in the past this process may have been all too sudden, it can now be a smoother, easier succession transition, where the BB can still contribute to the firm and retain status whilst taking a step back from the level of engagement they had previously. This approach is a healthier one for both the BB, their successor, and the firm.

As with other areas regarding Generation X, it is yet again squeezed between the old guard and the young thrusters. Having been managed by Boomers, there's a strong identification with the traditional work ethic and fear of being perceived as shirking or not applying oneself by being "present" or accessible at all hours. The BB machismo movement of being all about the work has left its mark on Gen X staff, who have grown to resent the time spent away from their young families and seeing the impact this attitude had on their parents' relationships. Now charged with bringing on the Millennial and Z generations, they are tempering views and starting to employ greater flexibility and latitude to the working day of their staff – but it's not an easy transition. As far as their own personal situation goes, Generation X is literally at a crossroads in thinking and planning. There will be those that cling on to the traditional views strongly held by BB's but the majority are now seeing the advantages of granting greater flexibility to the younger generations and relating this to how that might actually suit them.

We're moving beyond simple "dress down Fridays" to more impactful decisions such as increased homeworking. Gen X business owners need to experience the advantages and risks of employing new initiatives and there is no better way to do that than try it out for themselves. In this way they can appreciate where the younger staff are coming from in their appeal for such additional benefits and alternative working arrangements.

Examples:

- One or two days a month working from home;
- Four-day week;
- As many holidays as you want (just ensure the job is covered and performance not reduced);
- Duvet days as reward for performance;
- Flexi-time; and
- Job sharing.

I would recommend that any proposed initiative such as those above be tested by the executive team before implementing across the practice. In undertaking such assessments, the Gen X boss will gather essential information to help shape future policy and set guidelines on how best to manage such freedoms and flexibility.

Generation X staff will likely have older parents who require increased levels of attention and care, along with children who will be working their way through college and university, incurring all the associated costs and time demands that this stage of life throws up. Financially this can be a demanding and stressful period, with the need to find time to focus on their needs and not get lost in the cycle of caring up and down the generations without due care for their own wellbeing.

Promotion of mindfulness, fitness programs, and stress busting techniques can help educate staff to think more directly about their own needs. If demands on their time outside of work are such that they don't take due care, they can become unproductive and, worse, ill through increased stress. A proactive approach can help to head off such disruption.

Millennials were born for the work/life balance and the phrase "work to live, rather than live to work". It is life experiences that Millennials cherish, borne out by their desire for greater flexibility over bonuses. They need the freedom not to be shackled to a workstation and to be productive at home and on the move. A PwC survey identified that more than 60 percent of Millennials wish to spend greater time working from home and adjust their working hours. As Millennials increasingly take on management and ownership, we can expect to see the working pattern change further.

As for their leisure time, we all know that Millennials are associated with being the "life experience" generation and are never too far away from snapping that "killer" Instagram shot of reaching the mountain top, surfing, hiking in Peru, or shopping in Singapore. There is a risk of falling into such stereotypical thinking with all Millennials, but of course as humans we are all different.

What we do know is that Millennials have a healthier appreciation of the importance of their work in relation to their lives, health, and relationships. They're better connected socially and better informed of the need to strike a healthy work/life balance. It is this generation that is educating the previous BB's and X generations on how to manage a business in the 21$^{st}$ century. Of course, they won't always succeed in lobbying for greater flexibility or other direct benefits, but that won't stop them trying as, ultimately, they have confidence in their beliefs and a multitude of examples to support their arguments.

On a personal note, many Millennials will be in relationships and some will be experiencing the joy of parenting. With their own parents very often still in work and a little way off retirement, they'll need to rely on childcare, making time spent with their young ones precious, and often this can lead to a desire to make holidays all that more memorable. I sometimes reflect on the multitude of social media images of Millennial parents with their beautiful children in exotic and exciting locations and mentally fast forward to a time where those children will repeat the trips so they can truly experience it for themselves and take the parents along for the photo opportunity. Joking aside, Millennial leisure time is one of high expectation and shared experience, which in itself has created a peer group competition for achieving the highest level of Insta-gratification.

Early indications suggest that the newest generation at work – Gen Z – are more than ready for change. Nine to five seems an archaic concept in an era where they can be connected to anyone at any time, both through message and/or video and the talk of work/life balance has been around for decades with little sign of it being actioned. This generation could herald a quantum leap in our working lives and see a true harmonization of work and technology. Environmental and cost pressures could see the Gen Z desire matched to necessity, as commuting is harmful to the planet and use of homeworking an ideal way to reduce our carbon footprints.

When it comes to leisure pursuits, the Gen Z's have literally created whole new worlds for themselves. The environments themselves are not new – online gaming and YouTube have been around for many years – but Gen Z's have reinvented the mediums.

It was only relatively recently, within the last 12 months, that I discovered the world of Twitch, and a growing band of young people who are making very good money from broadcasting themselves playing online games such as Fortnite. The explosion of the dance phenomenon that was "the floss" is an outcome of this developing trend. A disclaimer here: not all Generation Z will be dedicated gamers, but there is certainly a very large proportion who are, or are alternatively dedicated to consuming broadcast entertainment from YouTube rather than traditional channels.

Smartphone proliferation and improved mobile/cell connectivity has further boosted these trends and this generation has been quick to seize on its capabilities. Many "older generation" commentators express concern for this latest age group but that is a cycle that has occurred over the years – we're always worried that we've broken a generation. The truth is that Gen Z's are resilient, better educated than any previous generation, and passionate about the issues that older generations have brushed under the carpet.

## Money

Baby Boomers – nearing or at retirement having suffered through the global recession – may be inclined to rethink thoughts of retirement to bolster their pension pots, protecting their lifestyle post-employment. This is of course not true for all BB's, but as a rule they will be more financially secure than their younger colleagues, having benefited from acquiring real estate and seeing its value accrue over the years. BB's and Gen X both face potential financial struggles with parents ageing and needing medical support and care, and children unable to acquire first homes, seeking financial support.

Moving toward or at the peak of their career, the X generation have children to put through education, possibly help into their first step into real estate, parents who are going to require increased care, and all this whilst trying to maintain a decent lifestyle of their own. Thoughts will be toward retirement in the mid-future and ensuring pension funds are at the correct levels. This is the generation under potentially the greatest financial pressure, post-recession.

It's been suggested that Millennials are less driven by financial gain and more interested in living "better lives" – but they still have needs to be met. Aspirational moves such as cars, holidays, and fashion support views that they need to match or better their peers to believe they are achieving their goals. With squeezed Gen X parents, Millennials seek to avoid the same traps and will not quickly commit to long-term investments such as mortgages or pensions, wary of the impact of the 2008 recession.

YouTube, Twitch, and Instagram influencers have shown the way for Generation Z on how fortunes can be made from passion projects and personal profiling. Of course, not everyone can achieve big bucks from such ventures, but "thinking differently" around income generation is a strong draw. As they develop their careers within the firm, Gen Z could potentially become frustrated quickly if they don't see progress happening fast enough. The Insta generation needs to feel it is being recognized and rewarded, no matter how modest the output may appear to their boss.

## Family

Baby Boomers have a strong affiliation with traditional family values and what constitutes a family unit. They may have difficulty acknowledging diversity, although this is less of an issue in the workplace as greater media emphasis has been made through various high-profile campaigns. BB's will feel committed to supporting and caring for elderly parents, which can take a greater amount of time akin to that of a new parent. As our population ages we will need to adjust thinking as to the time and leave afforded to staff dealing with end of life situations. Their offspring will be of an age where grandchildren may well be a factor and here again time to spend and offer support will be a factor and attraction toward greater flexibility.

As mentioned previously, Generation X have both ageing parents and children to deal with but the difference from BB's is that their offspring are younger and likely to still require more time and attention whilst their parents are more likely to be active and enjoying retirement or semi-retirement. Flexibility with their work time would also be welcomed by this generation, having an opportunity to work from home on a regular basis, potentially fewer hours so as to help with college selection, settling in and life after graduation, along with dealing with any life events that may be thrown their way.

Millennials can have some animosity toward the BB generation, who are likely to be their grandparents, due to their perceived wastefulness of resources and inability to respond to qualified reports of greenhouse gases and global warming. That said, family still looms large with this generation, who value tradition and marking events prominently on social media, be it trick or treating, thanksgiving, or birthdays. As this generation become parents, they will have a greater value for the time spent with children, unencumbered by the older generation's work ethic. This approach is changing the way maternity and paternity leave is handled and also in the increased flexibility for time required for events linked to children. It is important to draw a balance with those who may not have children and seek ways to offer a common benefit package, regardless of specific family circumstances. As an example, a member of staff may be a keen triathlete who travels the world to pursue their sport. That may be their passion, so potentially they could be granted additional leave matching that of a parent.

Generation Z has a strong connection to tradition but also to education of family members who are perhaps not yet informed on environmental, gender, or certain political views. This generation was born with the world literally at their fingertips; they're smart and enabled, but also passionate and loyal. They care for their family but equally have frustrations as to how quickly they are moving to address key issues.

## Passions and causes

When it comes to having a cause to support, the older generation has a stronger draw to campaigns driven by their church or religious leaders. There is also a strong altruistic tendency from senior partners who see the need to re-invest in their community. Cynics may argue that leaders who spend time working on various charitable projects are driven by the need to leave a legacy and concerns over the way in which their time and efforts are ultimately remembered. Of course, a desire for recognition is a human condition and if the pay-off is investment in worthy charitable ventures within the community, it's a win-win.

Seeing the world change so fast has been a challenge for the older generations, but Generation X has had to adapt faster than most. That added stress can often result in health-related issues and an awareness of how such factors affect colleagues. With ageing parents, X'ers will be conscious of the health risks and factors that may help to improve their quality of life into old age. X'ers are regular participants in events in which money is raised for chosen charities. These charities are often associated with causes close to their heart and those of family members, such as cancer research and hospice care.

Millennials are ready to tackle major political and economic issues head on, and having had 9/11 and school shootings impact their formative years they are driven to protect their own families and lifestyles. Community features strongly in many areas of a Millennial's life and working together for a mutual benefit is something this generation is quite adept at. The Arab Spring is an example of a Millennial-driven uprising where the use of social media and common spirit of addressing injustice drove huge numbers to protest and demand change.

Literally taking that community drive of the Millennials and raising it up a notch or four, the Gen Z's are fiercely engaged in their world and its future. Despair at the state in which they have found their world, global warming, failure of politicians, poverty, intolerance, and discrimination are all issues they face and are preparing to take on. We need this generation to repair the damage its predecessors have caused, and heroines such as Swedish schoolgirl and climate activist Greta Thunberg and Pakistani shooting victim and activist for female education, Malala Yousafzai, are two perfect examples of this new generation. With their example and others following suit, there is certainly hope for our world.

# Chapter 10: Ambition

In this chapter we will explore the drive and potential of those working for you and identify the subtle and perhaps not so subtle differences in approach to career progression.

It is important to not automatically confine Baby Boomers to a retirement "holding pattern". As we identified in chapter six on innovation, many entrepreneurs only found their career "secret sauce" well into their 50s and 60s. Yes, this generation were raised in the employment mode of head-down-and-work-hard, but not all will be waiting for a certain date to down work tools and replace them with garden implements.

There is an opportunity with BB's to offer ongoing developmental opportunities through upskilling. Technology and its applications is an ideal example and one where older members of staff can continue to feel valued by not being cast adrift by managers assuming they don't have an aptitude or appetite for change. This generation will still have a great deal to offer the business, and in keeping them engaged and motivated with opportunities for progression it sends a very strong message to the rest of the firm; you can succeed at any age.

For those Boomers who still have the fire of ambition burning bright, an opportunity to knowledge-share their newfound skills is an excellent way to both reinforce their learning and provide a developmental path as a trainer.

Although schooled and managed in their developmental phase by Baby Boomers, the X generation rebelled and sought to take personal control of their destiny. Not an exclusive trait of course but, in general, this age group brought a new confidence and drive to seek out and secure career opportunities, rather than considering a 40-year-long career with one employer as a mark of success. Not that there's anything wrong with dedicating your life to one employer; but through the 1980s and 1990s the commercial world evolved and a rise in competition, recessions, downturns, downsizing, and layoffs resulted in a far more unsettled workplace than that enjoyed by their predecessors.

Most Generation X employees will have devised a career plan which at this stage will be in its third or fourth edition, still seeking out those opportunities and keen to progress where possible. There will be those who have settled and are less focused, but in general terms we find this cohort to be at or very near the pinnacle of their career path. X'ers are a great asset for the firm – their experience and drive should be harnessed. Consider offering an insight to the strategic direction of the business, share its goals, and seek input. As with all staff there is a need to regularly appraise in a positive manner, but with an eye to avoiding potential apathy or over confidence that can prove costly faults in those who have long established careers within the firm.

One way to both play to experience and ego, as well as offer an assessment opportunity, would be to encourage internal presentations, putting forward an in-depth analysis of their area of expertise or thoughts on taking an area of the business forward.

The Millennial generation – which has driven the "work–life balance" campaign to a point where affirmative action has taken place – should not be considered any less interested in their career progression. Millennials are as ambitious as any generation that has preceded them, but their views on how they progress and what might qualify as "the right stuff" may not always be obviously in alignment with the partnership. The reason for the potential disconnect is the Millennial's interest in personal development and its connection with their role. Now that might sound rather obvious to many, but historically you would not always match personal growth with the job, believing instead that the role itself would develop you, the person, and any additional development would be in extracurricular activities. Millennials see their careers as fitting their lifestyle and their personalities in a way that actually makes a great deal of sense, but it is a subtle shift in emphasis that many managers can often read, incorrectly, as narcissistic behavior rather than a practical way to develop a career.

By way of an example, let's consider a Millennial employee who is an associate attorney in the employment law team. Their interests include working with diverse groups and helping them. They like their job but it's not fulfilling their needs and they're getting somewhat frustrated at the lack of interaction with others that their current role offers – mainly reviewing contracts of employment with little direct contact with clients. The head of the department discusses this need with the associate at their quarterly review and having reflected on the situation puts forward a proposal. The boss suggests that the associate spend two half-days a week working within the firm's HR department, where they can offer the benefit of their broader employment law knowledge and provide essential legal support to any internal matters that arise. They will also be charged with learning how the HR department functions and how it services the needs of the firm.

This suggestion may not be possible in all firms, but it is an example of applying lateral thought to help meet the needs of an employee whilst also adding value to the business.

The youngest of our generations have yet to spend long enough amongst us in the workplace to establish a strong differentiation from their Millennial cousins. Early indications are that whilst following their immediate predecessors in seeking personal growth within their chosen careers, the variation is in the time they may give an employer to realize their goals. "Stickability" is a term that may not apply too readily to Generation Z as they navigate the place of work and are confronted by traditional thinking and working practices. Having interviewed a large number of candidates of differing ages, genders, and levels over the years, I may need to address one of the resume filters that I apply. Historically, if I read a CV that highlighted a career journey with too many positions within a given period, I'd take the view that the candidate would be a risk, given the cost to induct and bring them up to a point of being truly productive. A logical conclusion, one would think. But now we find a generation that positively thrives on job hopping, all the time gathering all-important experience and skills. Generation Z may view a job held for two years as long enough and be very comfortable presenting themselves with a wide range of employers.

This generation may pose their future employers quite a challenge in keeping their attention and motivation, but if a firm can do this it will benefit from a very bright and capable age group. So how can employers tackle what they may see as "flighty" Z's who buzz into work then off again as quickly?

Not unlike the Millennials, Z's will seek fulfilment from their role and will want to know they are progressing. The key to unlocking their true potential and making a longer lasting connection could lie in the induction process and the culture of your firm.

## Measure of success

One way to assess staff capability and potential for progression is to create a plan for each employee, setting out the criteria by which they will be measured.

The simple act of presenting such a plan communicates a very positive, proactive message to staff who will appreciate the structure and clarity such a process can provide:

- A joint exercise – work through the plan together to agree the specific objectives and scope;
- Firm plans/objectives – share the current strategy and keep it updated;
- Skills audit – include a section to assess gaps in competencies and what the firm will do to help meet agreed learning needs;
- Annual action plan – set actions that are based on SMART objectives (Specific, Measurable, Achievable, Relevant and Time-scaled); and
- Monitoring process – don't overlook the all-important follow up sessions that should be scheduled regularly to ensure progress is on track.

## Promotion

When time comes to promote a member of staff, it's important that it is undertaken with the whole firm in mind and is consistent with its objectives.

No matter what age we are, we will always be boosted by progression and recognition of abilities and experience. If stepping up from assistant to full manager or taking on senior partner responsibility, BB's are likely to give the impression of taking it all in their stride. This coolness is due to the expectation they feel from others and a genuine fear of failure that applies to all but is buried more deeply by the older generation. With greater experience, BB's can make great candidates for promotion; however, they can also be set in a mode of working and managing that can prove out of step with the culture of your firm. Work on the "softer skills" analysis of any management position hire, and look at their emotional intelligence quotient and overall self-awareness. Being the oldest person on the shortlist certainly does not always translate as the wisest.

Nearing the peak of their careers, Generation X could be looking for that big break – the killer move that will make their career. Beware of the candidates who are desperately "reaching" and potentially going to fall foul of what is known as the "Peter Principle" – where an individual is promoted beyond their level of comfort and competence with disastrous consequences. On the upside you can find Gen X'ers to be driven, independently minded, and very capable, but if they are to be promoted to a position of managerial responsibility they will need the skills to get the very best out of two very different generations – Millennials and Generation Z. They will therefore need the skills to adapt their approach and seek to nurture the best within these age groups.

Millennials have been wrongly tagged as the "entitled" generation. Seeing a younger manager or department head promoted can be something of a problem for older generations. This is where maturity in candidates and a cross generational communication skill set is highly prized. All too often I have seen very bright and capable young managers have the career rug pulled from under them by older, resentful co-workers. It can be a very competitive environment in some firms and a level of Teflon toughness needs to be applied, along with empathy to understand such negative responses are borne out of their own fears and insecurities. We return to the all-important EQ – emotional intelligence.

In their early 20s, it's unlikely – although not impossible – for a Gen Z to be stepping up to the plate and taking on greater responsibility, along with an early promotion. To achieve such a step, it would be expected for the individual to have strong interpersonal skills and confidence. Noting the "stickability" point above, it may be a move to retain young talent that shows particular promise – but such early success can be a double-edged sword. The firm should ensure that the promotion of a Gen Z comes with its own care package of support and training to equip the individual for the role.

## Promotional opportunities

Here follow a few pointers that apply across the generations.

### The sudden vacancy

If faced with a short notice departure of a senior member of the team, take an opportunity to reflect before acting. Consider the reasons for the departure:

- Is the role necessary?
- Is it one or two-person position?
- Are the KPIs appropriate or in need of revision?
- Do you have an immediate replacement in-house?
- How urgent is the need to replace?

- Could you temporarily restructure to accommodate the tasks undertaken and take time to find the best candidate?

**The new position**

The firm has determined that a new role is required to fulfil an immediate market need. It requires a high-level candidate, potentially a partner.

- Review your current legal teams and identify any potential matches.
- Advertise internally.
- If an internal candidate applies but based on known evidence is too junior or simply inappropriate, be sure to follow a process whereby they are made aware why they may not be shortlisted without deflating their enthusiasm.
- If an identified candidate does not step forward, take the opportunity to have an informal discussion; they may be unaware of their standing with the partnership and lack a little confidence.
- Be sure to listen to feedback from candidates as there may be a common thread to concerns or demands regarding benefits that are not in line with other firms.

**The rising star**

An individual has shown themselves not only highly competent within the scope of their role but a natural leader and creative thinker.

- The traditional approach is to promote at the earliest opportunity to secure the talent for the firm. Before making such a move, talk to the individual and identify what their goals are, without scaring them off.
- If promotion is indeed the way forward, consider a staged promotion, potentially with a probationary period, where they can be afforded the opportunity to "try before they buy" the deal. There is nothing worse than making a decision in haste and discovering you've created a major headache for the firm.
- Be clear on what is expected and what success looks like for them and the firm and especially those who will be reporting to them.

**Tenure**

Negative disruption of a legal practice structure will have a direct impact on the performance of that firm, especially if the disruption is as a result of a departure or a series of leavers. If there is a revolving door of arrivals and departures it can seriously suck resource and cost simply finding replacements, let alone ensuring they're performing. The reputation of that firm can also be damaged through its lack of consistency in lawyer representation.

It can take an attorney a minimum of nine months to find their feet and start making a positive return for their new firm. More typically, it can be well in excess of a year – so imagine the impact if there is a rolling roll call of ever-changing faces.

The challenge to succeed as a successful law firm is to establish stability amongst the core and breed confidence through that stability. The employer can often feel like an extended family for those members of staff seeking certainty and figures to respect and look up to. If that trust is broken and the culture negative, it can lead to difficulties in attracting the right talent and ultimately leave the firm vulnerable.

More traditional in their outlook and relationship with their employer, Baby Boomers are loyal and prepared to knuckle down when things get tough but have little time for those who are not staying the course. According to the US Bureau of Labor, the average tenure of a Boomer is approximately ten years.

Generation X can be very loyal if the firm is supporting their career trajectory but will not endure poor management for long. They will more likely to try and find a way to shape the firm into their image for comfort if given the opportunity and will not stick around if the culture is not dynamic and ambitious.

Millennials will seek supportive culture and managers and will commit if the firm offers them personal development and career progression. They are more likely to keep an eye on vacancy posts and move on if a better opportunity presents itself, especially if the firm is not supporting their needs. The average tenure of a Millennial is 2.8 years.

Looking at the significant difference in average tenure between Baby Boomers and Millennials we do not see any reason to expect that shift to reverse. More likely, Generation Z's are even more unsettled than Millennials and it is a trend that will need careful management as greater numbers of these younger generations hold sway in the workforce.

Research by DeLoitte's 2019 Millennial Survey highlights the reasons for moving within two years.

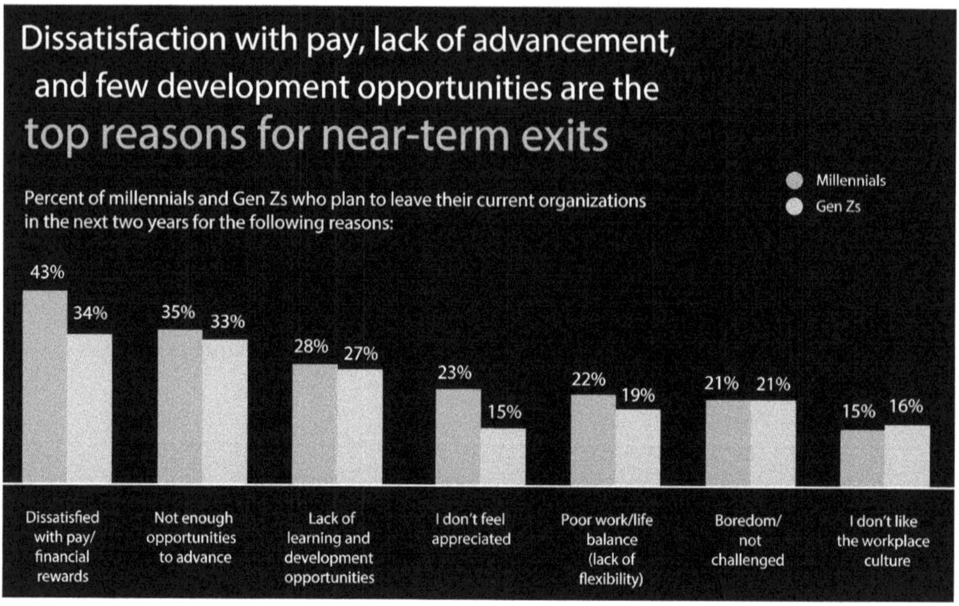


*Figure 1: Reasons for near-term exits. Source: Deloitte 2019 Millennial Survey.*

## Partnership and succession

Becoming a partner in a law firm is not always the big career step that many lawyers expected when first setting their sights on a career in the legal sector. Traditional partnership discussions involve investing in the firm by taking an equivalent of a second mortgage and buying an equity stake. More commonly now those first discussions are more of a first introduction to the title rather than business ownership via an offer of a role as a salaried partner.

Often, I hear managing and senior partners express concerns over where their next cohort of partners will come from. Increasingly, firms are finding it harder to source and retain their future owners and the cause of this drought in ambitious partnership-seeking attorneys is not something that can be easily addressed.

Millennials do not lack ambition, but they do have a healthy regard for risk and reward. They understand that the traditional partnership route can take time, typically taking incremental steps in equity acquisition. This investment is not cheap, and the financial returns are often not as clear cut and lucrative as they once were.

Whereas historically there would be a pick of the firm's talent lining up eager and wanting to be chosen for the award of partnership, we now face a far harder "sell" of the role. For a number of firms, the pitch and drive to recruit future leaders is not hitting the mark and leaving the "old guard" in post just getting older!

Without an effective plan for succession in place, the mid- to long-term future of practices is in jeopardy. The Millennial generation want to know that the firm they work in is planning ahead and securing its future. In the past the partnership didn't worry about taking such measures as it wasn't seen as an issue but now it's a problem if you don't have a plan.

Creating a plan is not as straightforward as it may sound, and it would be worth looking at recent history for examples of when it worked and – just as important – times your best efforts at succession failed. Be honest with yourself and look at the facts. Seek out a process that engages with the main players at the earliest possible opportunity and allows for regular and consistent communication. Managing expectations will be critical, from the young aspirational lawyer who believes partnership equals big bucks to the Baby Boomer partner worried about her pension and income at the point of retirement.

## Career planning

The process of identifying the future leaders and owners of the business should start at the point of recruitment. Of course, not everyone will make partner or be considered in a long list but identifying those with potential and nurturing that talent must be seen as a key priority.

Examples of what to look for:

- A good grasp of business finance;
- Excellent client-facing skills;
- Income generation;
- Strong interpersonal skills;
- Good rapport with senior and junior colleagues; and
- Innovative thinking.

Set your own list of desirable attributes and identify those individuals who demonstrate their potential to meet the partnership model for your firm.

Create an annual program of development with opportunities for:

- Cross-departmental secondments;
- Projects designed to stretch;
- Mentoring for prospects and opportunities for them to act as mentors;
- Presentation and public speaking opportunities; and
- Involvement in strategic matters and working with senior partners.

### Client care succession

Whilst prospective partner candidates are clearly important to this process, they are not the exclusive focus when thinking of succession planning. It is highly likely that your firm will have a number of clients that should be involved in the "handover". The sudden announcement of a new contact without a measured and planned introduction could cause concern and potentially a threat to that relationship.

To avoid any client fears or opportunities for competitors to step in and steal the account, you should involve them in your succession process. What is critical here is timing. If you introduce them too soon the new partner may not prove to be a long-term fit and the handover prove premature; if too late the client may feel "out of the loop" and not considered important enough to be kept aware of developments.

### Retirement planning

Understandably there has been a great deal of focus on the prospective new partner – but what of those who are making way to create the space for the new partner? Having held a position of considerable responsibility and status, it can be something of a shock to the system to be suddenly no longer the focal point or go-to person in the firm.

Careful management and planning for those who are nearing retirement is a very important part of ensuring success with succession. In the run up to the handover, the partner stepping down should be permitted to contribute thoughts on their next phase with the firm. Some may wish to retire completely and move on to new projects, others preferring to continue in a consultancy role. The call ultimately will be that of the management board but there can be distinct advantages to retaining the knowledge and connections associated with these ex-partners. With longer and healthier lifespans it should be possible for many older partners to stay in touch and add value long past their official retirement date.

## Ongoing management and measurement

As with any management process created within the firm, you should always check-in to make sure it is working, relevant, and delivering the right outcomes for the practice. Succession is a complex, often overlooked or misunderstood aspect of running a successful legal practice. In part, it is frequently overlooked as those who are in line for stepping down would rather not think of that day, and when matters are personal, logic and subjectivity can be in short supply. The key to successful succession is in placing the responsibility in the hands of those outside the direct line of involvement, such as a VP or director of HR.

# Chapter 11: Leadership

A successful business needs strong, capable, and visionary leadership, but securing such resources to help grow a law firm can prove something of a challenge.

Historically, you may have selected the next leaders of the firm through a democratic vote amongst the entire firm or just the equity partners and executive board. Alternatively, selection may have been as simple as picking the partner who has been in post the longest, or who is simply the most popular and considered a "safe pair of hands".

Making such important decisions can be as difficult as electing the leader of a political party or a country – and we know how that can often turn out. There is an art and science to apply to this process that will help you identify those with "the right stuff" – but of course there can rarely be any guarantees that you'll achieve your stated objectives simply by making one or two high level recruitment decisions.

Whoever takes on the challenge of running and leading the firm will need a strong team around them, and essentially a detailed and well-designed strategic plan to work to.

In generational terms, the age of the Baby Boomer boss is coming to a natural end and the Generation X leaders in their 40s to mid-50s are most likely to be the prevalent age group taking the reins. Let's not overlook the up and coming Millennials who by number outweigh the X Generation. There are a growing number of highly effective and entrepreneurial leaders born in the 1980s making a significant impact in the world of business, with many featuring digital technologies in their career journeys and stories of success:

- Alexia Bonatsos, venture capitalist and former co-editor of TechCrunch – age 37;
- John Zimmer, co-founder and President of Lyft – age 35; and
- Julia Hartz, CEO and co-founder of Eventbrite – age 39.

Relying on the older generation to safely navigate the firm through the next decade may work but equally it could be risky given the speed of change in the way we are working, and consumer behaviors. At the very least, those responsible for leading their firms need to access and be prepared to listen and act on information they can gather on emerging trends and events that are likely to impact on the future prosperity of their business.

A famous quote from Nelson Mandela on leadership:

> *"A leader is like a shepherd. He stays behind the flock, letting the most nimble go out ahead, whereupon the others follow, not realizing that all along they are being directed from behind."*

## Methods and styles

I suspect we have all experienced working in a business where there was one autocratic, controlling and overpowering "boss" – not so much shepherd as acting like a wolf. These individuals ruled with an iron fist and insisted on having things their way, seeing any alternative view as a challenge to their authority. It might sound far-fetched if you've not had the pleasure, but such leaders do indeed exist and some still retain those positions of power and influence – albeit thankfully they are fast becoming an endangered species.

The reason for the demise of the dictator manager is that in today's law firm such behavior will swiftly leave the individual isolated and struggling to command the respect and required response from their workforce. Gen X and certainly Millennial and Gen Z employees will not endure such a traditional, hierarchical command and control management method and will ultimately vote with their feet, seeking a job where they will feel valued and secure.

Effective leadership requires a combination of personality, aptitude, and technique capable of engendering loyalty, enthusiasm, and effort amongst their employees. Where it can often fall down is where a newly appointed manager, VP, or managing partner adopts a "persona" to help deliver their message. This is something I've witnessed firsthand as an individual behaves in a manner they believe to be appropriate for the new position but in the process leave behind their natural personality. This may sound odd if you've not encountered such a metamorphosis, but it is quite common and something to be avoided at all costs.

Your staff are not blind to the challenges faced by a leader – but neither are they blind to insincerity borne out of adopting a different stance and style simply because their job title has changed.

There is no "one size fits all" leadership model but by far the most effective approach is one that draws on aspects within the existing make-up of the personality. We are all human and thereby not perfect, so being self-aware and able to work on any areas that are in need of refining will be seen as positives and a strength of the individual rather than a weakness. One very common example is public speaking. It's remarkable how many make it to very senior roles yet have failed to tackle presentation skills. No one is expecting a slick stand-up comedian or JFK oration, but rambling, stumbling, and lack of engagement with an audience will count against them. Again, the approach should be to use the platform of the personality and build from that foundation.

When we look at the specific categories of leadership style the most popular fall into seven distinct types.

**1. Autocratic**
A single, top down management style that seeks little if any feedback other than support for their actions.

**2. Democratic**
The polar opposite, this leader will look for consensus and agreement from others to verify the path taken. This leader works well in most organizations as long as communication is clear and engagement of key decisions undertaken with the right individuals.

**3. Coach**
A leader who can get the best out of teams, encourage, identify opportunities and work collaboratively to achieve goals. These leaders tend to be very "hands on" with projects and visible throughout the business.

**4. Strategic**
One who can effectively communicate a business plan and work with individuals who are, as a consequence, motivated to deliver it.

**5. Transformational**
A dynamic leadership style often associated with fast moving businesses with demanding objectives to meet. This leader is able to accept challenging situations and coordinate resources to hit targets.

**6. Laissez-faire**
There's an argument that suggests that if you get the recruitment piece

right, a leader has effectively achieved their goal. Letting staff get on with their jobs, not interfering or directing is the style of this leader.

### 7. Charismatic/personality led

A leadership style we can all recognize – the face of the company and someone who will attract others in as investors, partners, or employees through their charm and guile. A downside to this style of leadership is the organization's association with an individual and the risks that this may introduce to the business.

Not unlike our individual personalities, there are times when we can be any one of the above, even the autocrat if it's a bad day. The opportunity for strong and effective leadership rests with those placed in positions of authority who can best adapt to any given circumstance, have clarity in vision and communication, engage with their employees, be genuine in their approach, and consistent in the delivery of their message.

## Culture

Building trust is hugely important for a leader to be effective. Edelman's 2019 Trust Barometer[1] highlighted the shift in employees' trust from traditional authority figures such as government and NGOs to employers.

This places a considerable responsibility on organization leaders at a time when many amongst the Millennial and Gen Z age groups are questioning the efficacy of business – both those that they buy from and those they work with.

There are considerable fears at this time concerning personal security, jobs, discrimination, debt, economic uncertainty and not least the environment and the steps required to ensure the planet remains habitable for the generations to come.

With the above in mind, it is becoming increasingly apparent that firms who are seen to not only acknowledge such factors but actively move positively toward addressing these fears will win favor with existing and future employees. Apathy and ambivalence will not cut it with the Millennial and Z generations who will not wish to work for, instruct, or supply an organization that fails to have robust policies covering these issues.

Leaders are fast coming to terms with the need to develop an inclusive and caring culture and to engage directly with the younger members of their company in order to achieve this.

A stand-out item from the Edelman Trust Barometer 2019 is the dramatic increase in trust toward the employer away from government, media, or general business community. We are more trusting of our employers, not least because of the lack of trust in alternatives such as politicians who are seen to have failed the public.

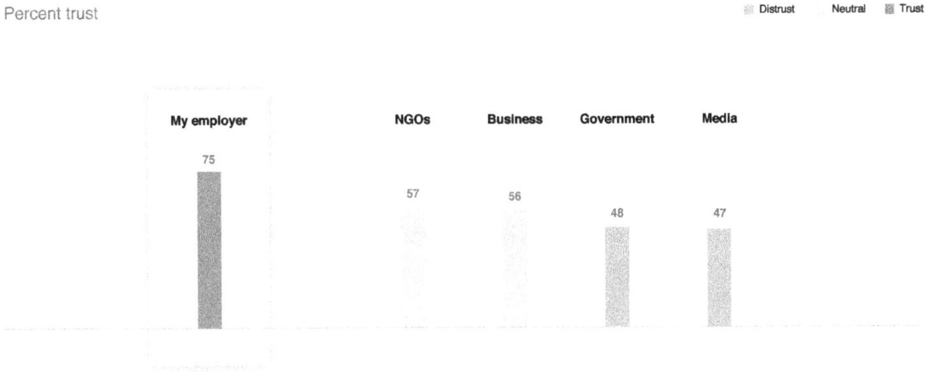


*Figure 1: Most trusted relationship. Source: Edelman Trust Barometer 2019.*

A direct consequence of this increase in trust is the expectation that CEOs will be the ones to lead the fight for change. Seventy-six percent say they want CEOs to lead change instead of waiting for government decisions. Seventy-three percent also expect their employer can improve their outlook, both for their job security by increasing profitability but also impact on social conditions within their community.

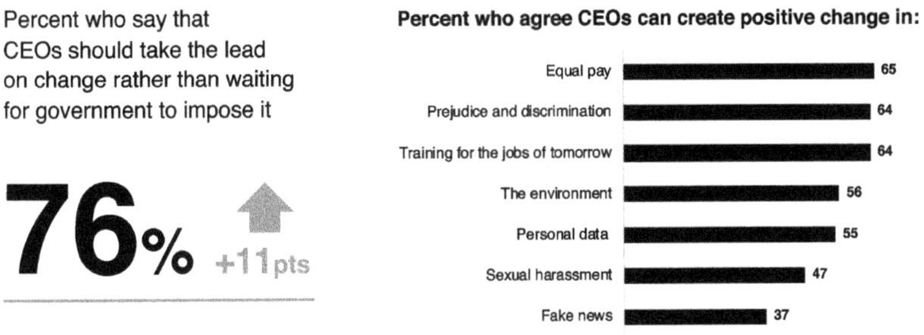


*Figure 2: Leadership from CEOs. Source: Edelman Trust Barometer 2019.*

Employers who actively engage in such social, community support can expect to see greater commitment (83 percent), testimony (78 percent) and loyalty (74 percent) from employees.

The leaders in these employer organizations will be expected to lead on change within their communities as well as paying direct attention to values, future, purpose, and operational matters.

## Activities

### Innovation

The legal sector has on more than one occasion been accused of sticking its head in the sand and ignoring the world as it changes around it. The truth today is that no business, no matter its pedigree or tradition, can afford to stand still, let alone plant its face in the ground.

One example of such current stasis and procrastination in the face of obvious and potentially radical change is the introduction of Blockchain technology and smart contracts. It is relatively new technology, but fast being adopted by governments and financial institutions across the globe. In the UK a working party set up by the Law Society has had the technology under review for almost two years. At the point at which they were due to announce their findings a second group, the LawTech Delivery Panel, backed by the government, announced it was launching a consultation process. This second group has now taken up the mantle for the sector in the UK, begging the question as to what the Law Society group achieved.

Whilst it's a positive step to review such emerging and established technologies, the lack of urgency and crossover in bodies aiming to deliver certainty has not helped law firms in the UK who could find themselves playing catch up to a series of businesses that have already developed applications meeting the needs of existing clients.

Leaders need to be alive to such innovations and be agile in thinking, ideally being at least one step ahead rather than behind the trend curve.

### Recognition

Rewarding staff for their efforts and thanking clients for their business and suppliers for their support may seem a pretty straightforward act but its often one overlooked in the hurly burly, hectic world we currently inhabit. Good leaders know when to recognize the contribution of others as no success is down to one individual or one team.

### Take decisive action

There can be occasions when the leader is faced with conflicting arguments for a strategic move, potentially a merger with another practice. The job of the leader is to ensure they have the best possible intelligence so as to make an appropriate judgement call. The impact of any decision can be far reaching but prevaricating or procrastinating when you're furnished with all the facts will not help the business.

### Be prepared to be unpopular

Some very well-meaning managers can fall into the trap of seeking approval and recognition from their staff instead of respect born out of clear leadership. At times your decisions may prove unpopular but, in the long run, if taken for logical commercial reasons, the team will see why such steps are taken.

The truth is that you will fail if you try and keep everyone happy – that is simply an impossible task – but as long as your decision-making is based on rational thinking and with the business in mind, without undue harm to others, it should not be open to undue criticism. That said, the ability to handle criticism and not take matters personally is a critical attribute of an effective leader.

### Use humor

Where appropriate, and without making light of serious issues, a sense of humor can help deal with conflicts and disputes between colleagues and departments. Of course, sensitivity is necessary, but if used effectively it can convey confidence and help put matters into perspective, lightening a dark mood.

### Deadlines

Whatever the strategy, it will have its objectives, and achieving these will be accomplished through the delivery of a number of actions or projects. Without clearly set out, communicated, agreed and realistic deadlines you'll be making tasks harder to manage. Deadlines are critical to focusing minds and resource to reaching targets.

## Strategy

As a leader, it's as important to determine what is out of scope as well as what you can expect to achieve. Managing expectations is critical as over promising and stating you'll achieve six goals will end up looking like failure if only three are reached, despite their importance.

At the outset of any planning, take time to assess the business priorities and where you are going to be best placed to spend valuable time and resource in achieving a goal.

For example, you may have an established area of the firm that's underperforming and one that has huge potential but little direction. You have time for one of these opportunities. Which should you focus on?

The answer is of course not straightforward and will always be nuanced with personal stories, preferences, and an historical narrative around the way the firm has handled such matters in the past. The way to decide is to look at the opportunity and reward versus cost and risk. What will happen if you don't take on one of the projects? Is there an alternative option?

Depending on the profitability of the practice, an area that is costing money due to underperformance may take on greater importance than it would for a firm that is performing well and is profitable.

Consider applying tried and tested models such as the Boston Consulting Matrix to focus on specific areas of the business. Use these models to help determine those areas that you feel offer the greatest net financial returns and would benefit from your lead and attention as opposed to those that present the least attractive payback. There's no harm in being ambitious, but nothing worse than over stretching your leadership team and falling short.

## Communication

Whatever the plans are, they must be clearly communicated to those you consider would benefit from the detail. Increasingly, firms are sharing their top-level plans with ALL staff in an effort to garner collective understanding and motivation toward achieving the goals.

As progress is made throughout the year it's always helpful to keep staff broadly appraised of where the firm is on its strategic path. This will help to keep any rumor mill quiet and re-focus attention if extra effort is required from specific areas.

### *Reference*

1. Research and graphic courtesy of the Edelman Trust Barometer 2019: www.edelman.com/trust-barometer

Chapter 12:
# The next generation

## Future generations

If we track the life experiences of a member of the silent generation, who will now be close to if not already retired (age 75+), we can see the journey they've been on since the end of the Second World War.

Would they have known that in their lifetime their experiences would include McCarthyism, the Cold War, access to 24/7 television and online news coverage, the Civil Rights Act, JFK's assassination, a space race and moon landing, Vietnam, Watergate, economic booms, the Berlin Wall coming down, the Arab Spring, 9/11, ISIS, the global banking crisis, technological explosion, reality TV, social media and #MeToo?

The above provides a few examples of the events that have fallen within the living memory of one generation but, typically, those that impact early life have the greatest effect. It's these years that shape approach and attitudes.

So, what of future generations? Let's start with Gen Z.

## What do we know?

They've only ever known a world connected by the internet, and as soon as they were old enough to wield a smartphone or tablet they could do so, with the added attraction of social media apps.

As we better understand the technology and its effect on our lives and in particular our thinking, it's becoming increasingly clear that whilst many benefits come with such advances, the payoff can be somewhat damaging. Teens using apps that bring harassment, bullying, and at times worryingly dark thoughts have highlighted the less palatable side of social media.

Facebook's evolution over the last 15 years has seen it enter into controversial territory concerning privacy and data usage,[1] getting the social media giant in hot water with governments concerned over its impact on democracy.

They have also witnessed an increasingly erratic and unpredictable political scene with Donald Trump's "Make America Great Again" campaign, his "Wall", and alleged collusion with Russia. Missile testing, continued terror attacks, and random shootings notably in schools across America would make the most robust character somewhat anxious – and guess what? Anxiety-related conditions are on the increase.

Unhelpfully, the term "Snowflake Generation" seems to have been adopted by older generations to accuse Gen Z's of failing to cope with life's occasional hurdles and pushing back when they don't like what they see or hear. In 2016 the *Collins Dictionary* made the term "Snowflake Generation" one of its words of the year.

We only need to step back one more generation to see how the same criticism was made of Millennials. In China, the term "Strawberry Generation" was applied to imply that, as with the fruit, this age group was protected, allowed to grow without any harm, limited from exposure to life's trying events and as a result were easily bruised when, in adulthood, they faced challenges.

Is this labelling fair? Not in my opinion. The world is changing very fast, faster than at any other point in our history, driven by increases in population, mobility, environmental concerns and of course communication, and the inter-connectivity offered by technology. It will be the Gen Z's who take on the responsibility of navigating through significant global issues, so forgive them their furrowed brows and at times short temper; the older generations didn't act particularly responsibly when it came to the world's resources and now they will need to come up with the answers.

Projecting beyond the Z generation is hard to call, but if we take an optimistic view of our future we can see that they could preside over a paradigm shift in our political, economic, and essentially environmental approach. Perhaps we'll start being kinder to each other and find ways to heal some of those long held, bitter feuds between nations, races, religions, and genders.

The older generations should support the new arrivals and let them find their way forward without undue interference or abuse.

If the Z's broadly succeed in protecting the planet and prevent a dystopian 21$^{st}$ century they will offer a strong lead to the generation that follows. It's likely that lessons learnt of ecology and economic sustainability will be passed on.

**Planning**

Back to the here and now – what can you do to prepare for what may be around the corner?

We've covered a number of the key strategies and development opportunities that will help to engender a more cohesive firm with cross-generational collaboration. Many senior executives and owners talk about their businesses as being like an extension of their family. At times this can sound contrived but, in reality, with such a breadth of ages working in "relative" (see what I did there?!) proximity it's something to aspire to. That is if the aspiration is a happy, supportive, nurturing and dynamic family unit, rather than a dysfunctional group of individuals harboring long-held grudges and with a single-minded focus on self.

Recruit to meet the needs of the firm with a focus on the cultural match of the candidate's personality. Train and develop staff using methods that best suit their learning preferences rather than apply a single one-size-fits-all approach.

Communicate with clients in terms and methods that they prefer and are comfortable with; sometimes the latest technology is not the solution. Manage by insisting on consistency of goal setting and common understanding of what the goals are and how they are to be met. Offer flexibility where appropriate and be open to new suggestions, albeit keep an eye on the quality of the output and productivity. Offer mentoring throughout the practice and be inclusive, noting it's often said empty vessels make the most sound, so by contrast quieter members of staff may have something very interesting to share. Measure, analyze performance, and reward success on a collective rather than individual basis.

Encourage innovation and don't discount older generations from the conversation; they too can have new ideas.

As new technology is introduced, encourage champions from ALL generations and ensure the benefits are clearly understood as well as the features.

The desire to have an alternate income stream and "insurance policy/ life raft" source is a natural consequence of the economy we live in. Don't let it interfere with the day job but be open to allowing staff to share their ventures and support them.

When "out of office" remember staff will have many and varied interests and – depending on the generation – priorities. Whilst not being intrusive it's always useful to understand the motivations and passions of staff as there may be hidden talents that you could make use of.

Traditional views on ambition and career progression have changed and no longer can you expect the same conveyor belt of eager lawyers all wanting to be partner. Now the challenge is to find the approach that will attract the brightest and best to take on the responsibility. Understanding the way in which Millennials and Gen Z think will be essential for successful succession.

Effective leadership is a long way removed from the traditional authoritarian approach and now an inclusive and nurturing approach is the way to both motivate and retain the necessary talent pool for a firm that aims to grow.

Capably managing generational diversity in a law firm or any business will prove to be an increasingly important goal. If there is a failure to bring the business together and respect each grouping it can undo a great deal of planning and effort by senior managers and executive boards.

By implementing an effective strategy, from recruitment to retirement, the firm will be better placed to reap the rewards of engaging a generationally diverse workforce.

### *Reference*

1. Cambridge Analytica and links to Facebook's involvement in the impact on voting in the 2016 EU Referendum.

www.ingramcontent.com/pod-product-compliance
Ingram Content Group UK Ltd.
Pitfield, Milton Keynes, MK11 3LW, UK
UKHW021834131026
9310IPUK00004B/75

9 781783 583768